AF604273

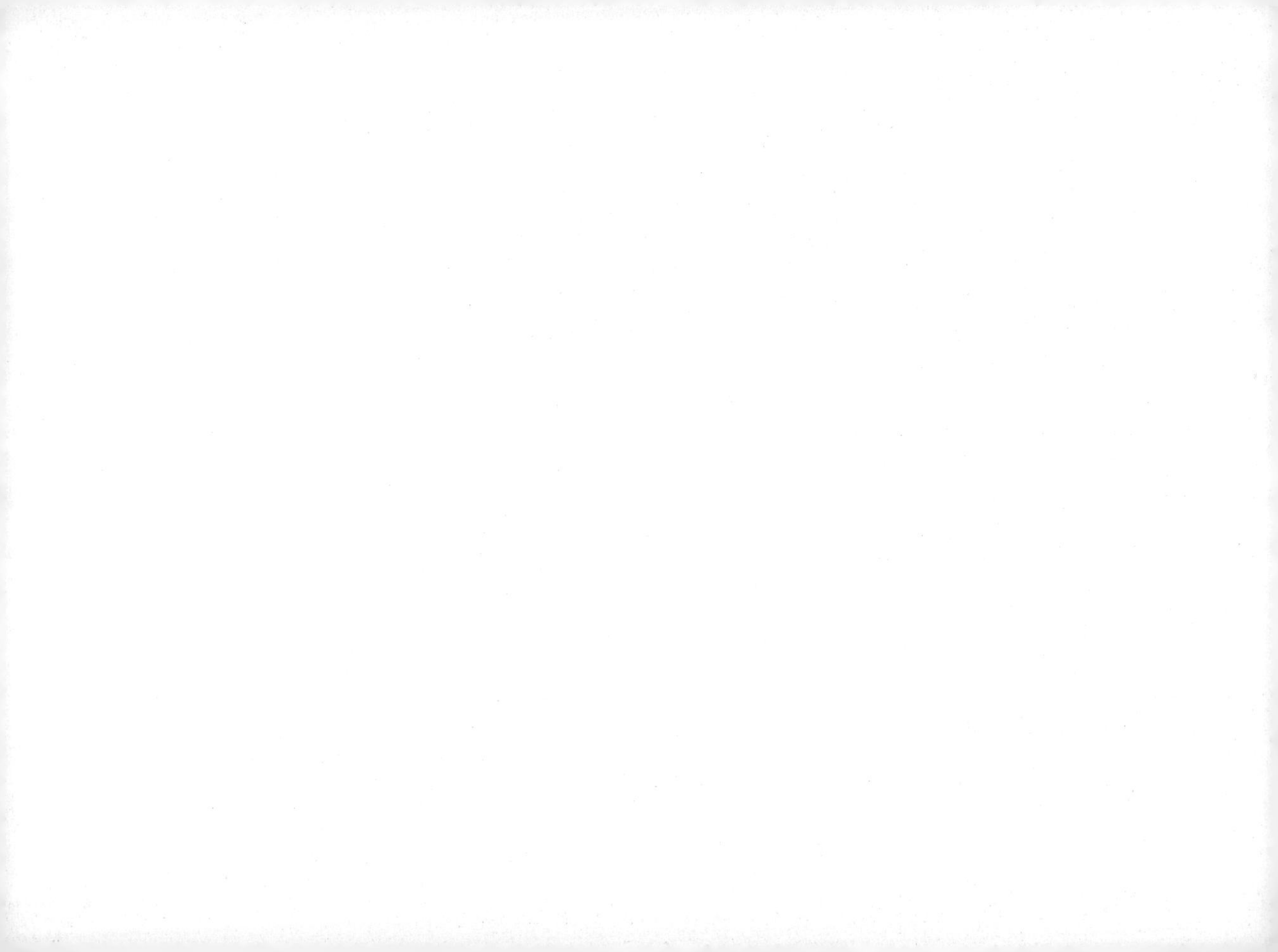

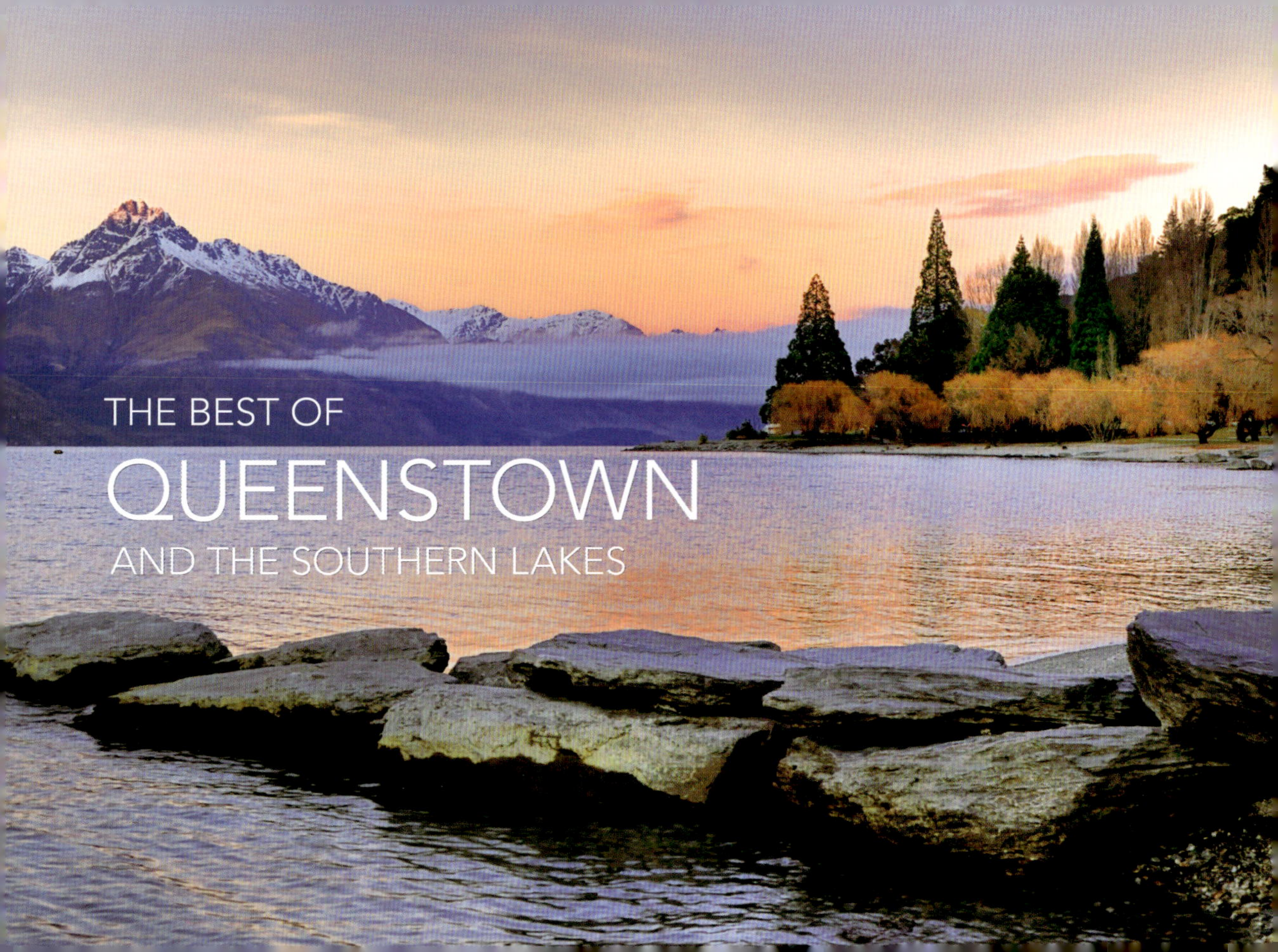

THE BEST OF

QUEENSTOWN

AND THE SOUTHERN LAKES

Published in 2022 by David Bateman Ltd
Unit 2/5 Workspace Drive, Hobsonville, Auckland 0618, New Zealand
www.batemanbooks.co.nz

ISBN 978-1-98-853836-5

Book design: Catherine Wells, Kōtare Design
Printed in China by Everbest Printing Co. Ltd

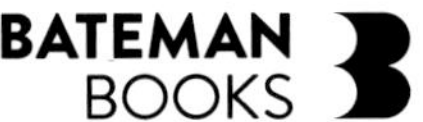

Previous page: Morning, Lake Wakatipu

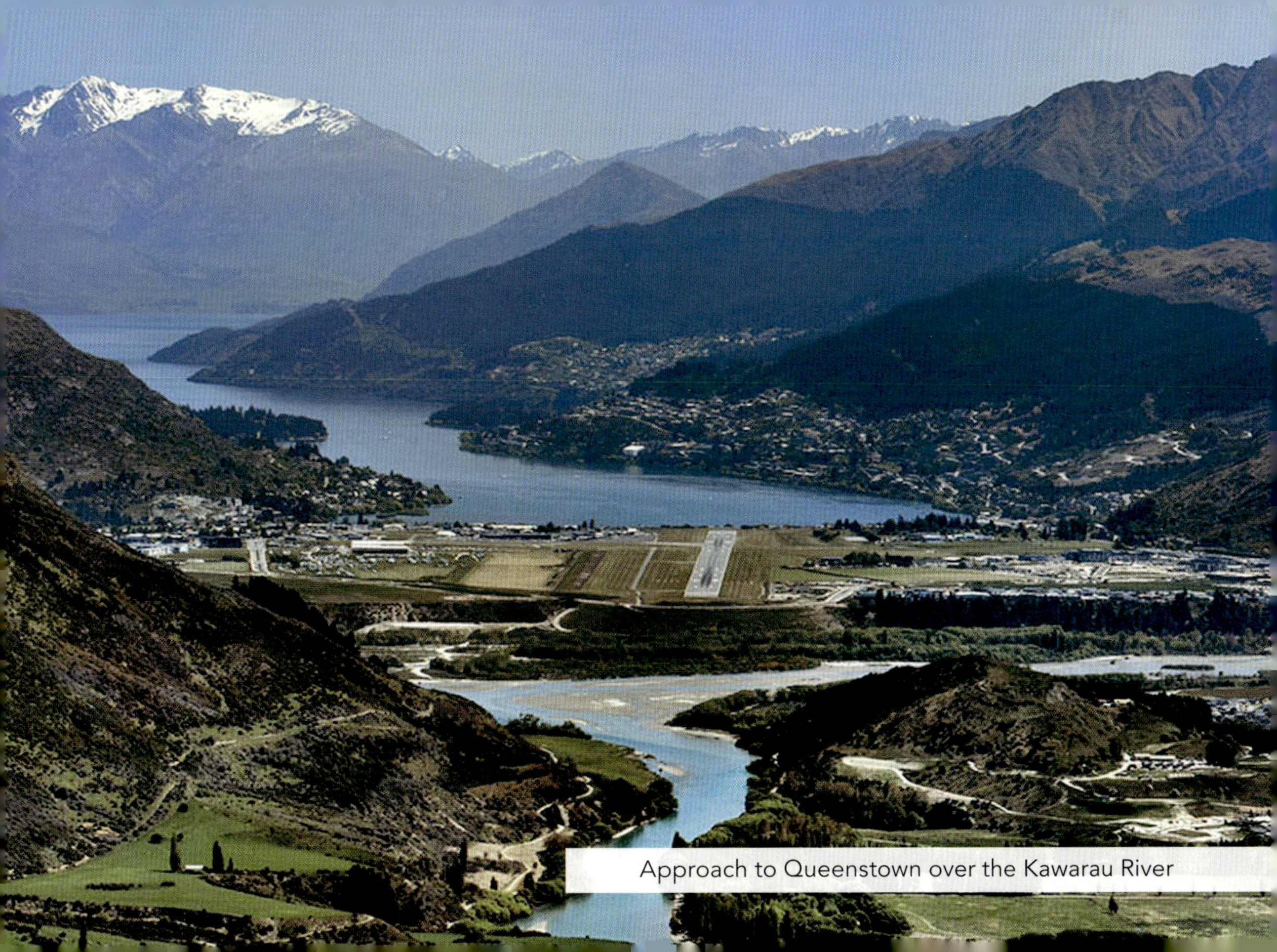

Approach to Queenstown over the Kawarau River

This book takes you on a journey through the south-western part of the South Island, Queenstown and southern lakes area — a region of impressive mountains, picturesque lakes, dramatic fiords, rolling pastures and rugged beaches.

Known as the Adventure Capital of the World, Queenstown is home to the original Bungy jump from the Kawarau River Bridge. Along the northern shore of Lake Wakatipu, surrounded by beech forests and awe-inspiring mountain ranges, is the settlement of Glenorchy, gateway for several of New Zealand's renowned multi-day walks.

North-east of Queenstown reveals the abandoned goldmining areas of Skippers Canyon, Macetown, and the delightful heritage gold-rush village of Arrowtown. Further on through the Cardrona Valley is the Wānaka area. For Māori, this was a natural crossroads. Highway 6, through Haast Pass, in the Te Wāhipounamu World Heritage area, follows the ancient pathway, Tioripatea, one of many trails used for hunting and collecting the highly valued pounamu (greenstone).

South of the Wānaka area lies the Cromwell Basin where the remnants of goldmining lie amongst vineyards and orchards. Cromwell township, originally known as 'The Junction', sits on the shores of the man-made Lake Dunstan.

Originally, Cromwell was located at the confluence of the Clutha River / Mata-Au and the Kawarau River. The junction was notable for the water colour difference between the two rivers. In the early 1990s construction of the Clyde Dam and the creation of Lake Dunstan drowned the river confluence and the township was moved to its current site.

After skirting Lake Dunstan and following the Kawarau River through the dramatic Kawarau Gorge, Highway 6 runs south along the shores of Lake Wakatipu to Kingston continuing further south to Invercargill.
At the village of Five Rivers, the journey passes south-west through small settlements and the rolling landscape of Southland to Te Waewae Bay on the Fouveaux Strait coast.

Further west, partially surrounded by the Kepler and Murchison Mountains are Lakes Manapouri and Te Anau within Fiordland National Park, part of the Te Wāhipounamu World Heritage Area. At the northernmost point of Lake Te Anau is the entrance to the Milford Track.

Highway 94 (the Milford Road), from Te Anau, passes through the stunning landscapes of the Eglinton Valley and follows another traditional Māori pathway over the mountains to the spectacular Milford Sound / Piopiotahi.

At the end of the book are maps showing the vantage points where many of the images are located.

Queenstown

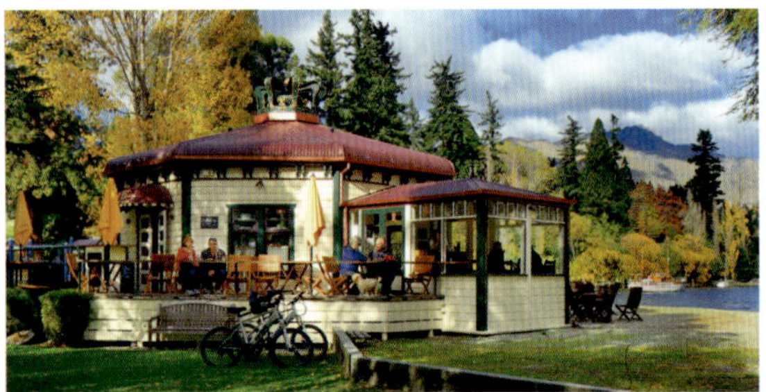

Restored Coronation Bathhouse

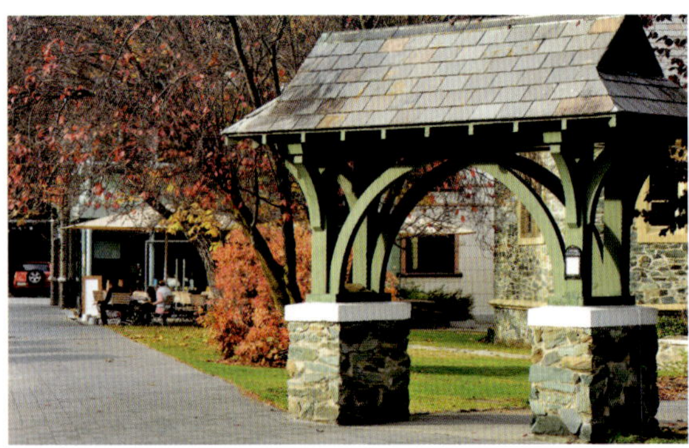

St Peter's Church Gate

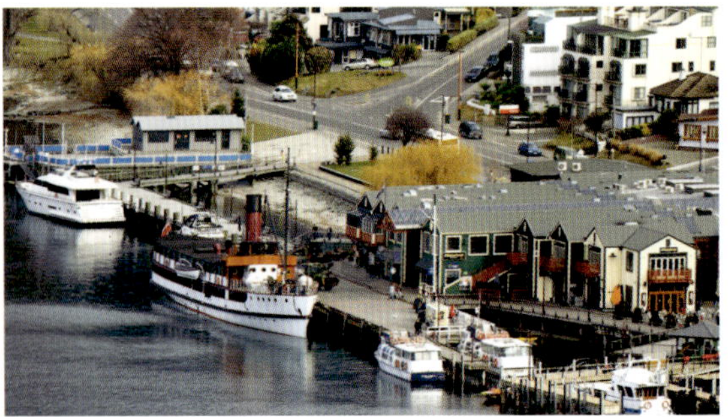

SS *Earnslaw* alongside Steamer Wharf

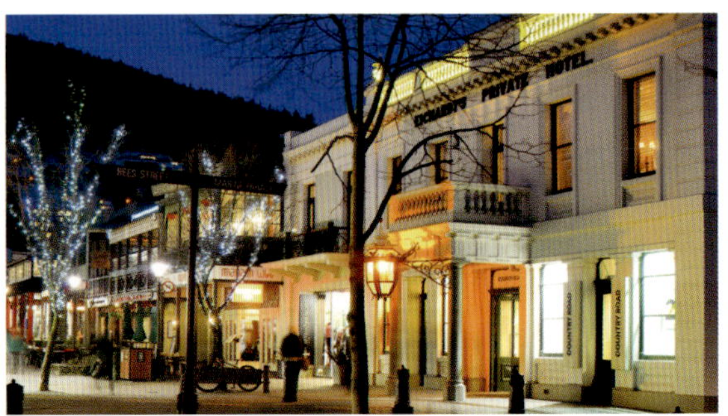

Historic Eichardt's Hotel

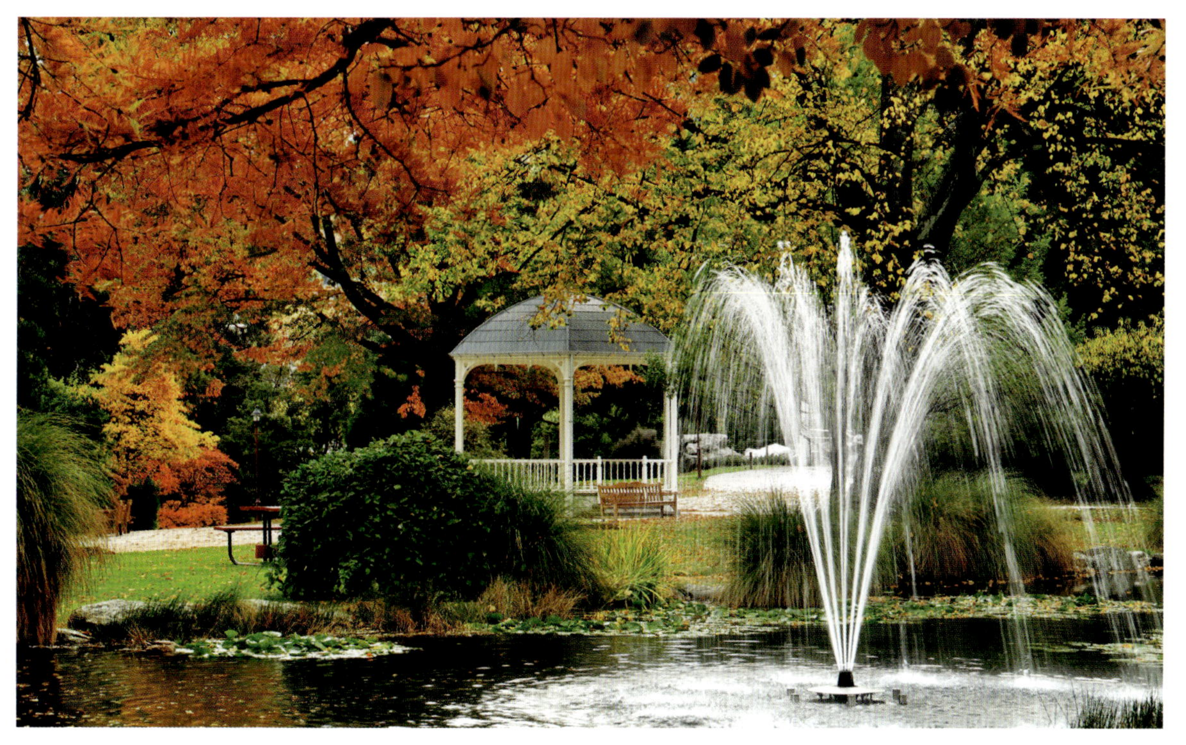

Queenstown Gardens

Queenstown – Glenorchy Road

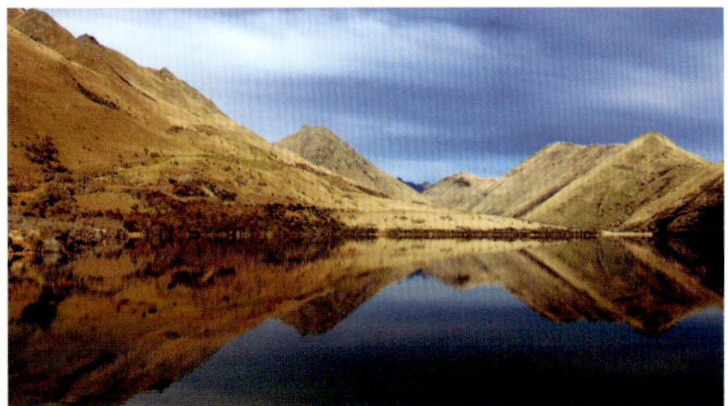

Moke Lake

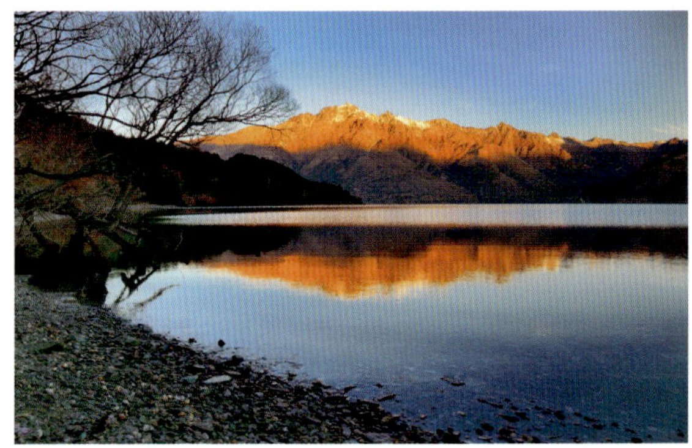

Wilson Bay

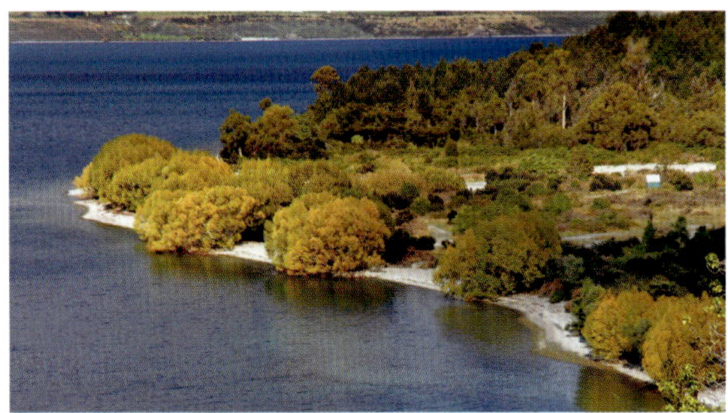

12 Mile Delta

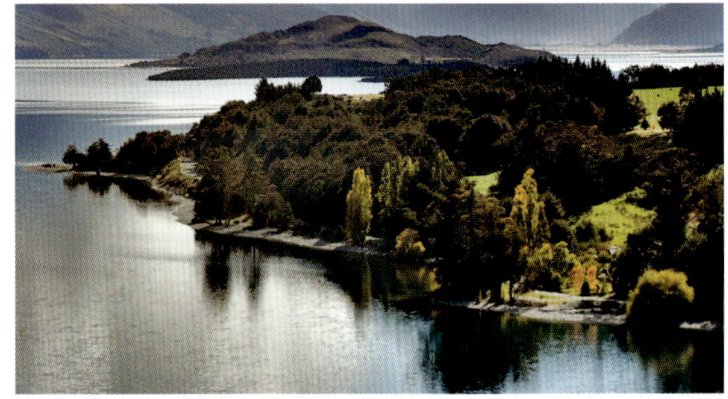

Meiklejohns Bay

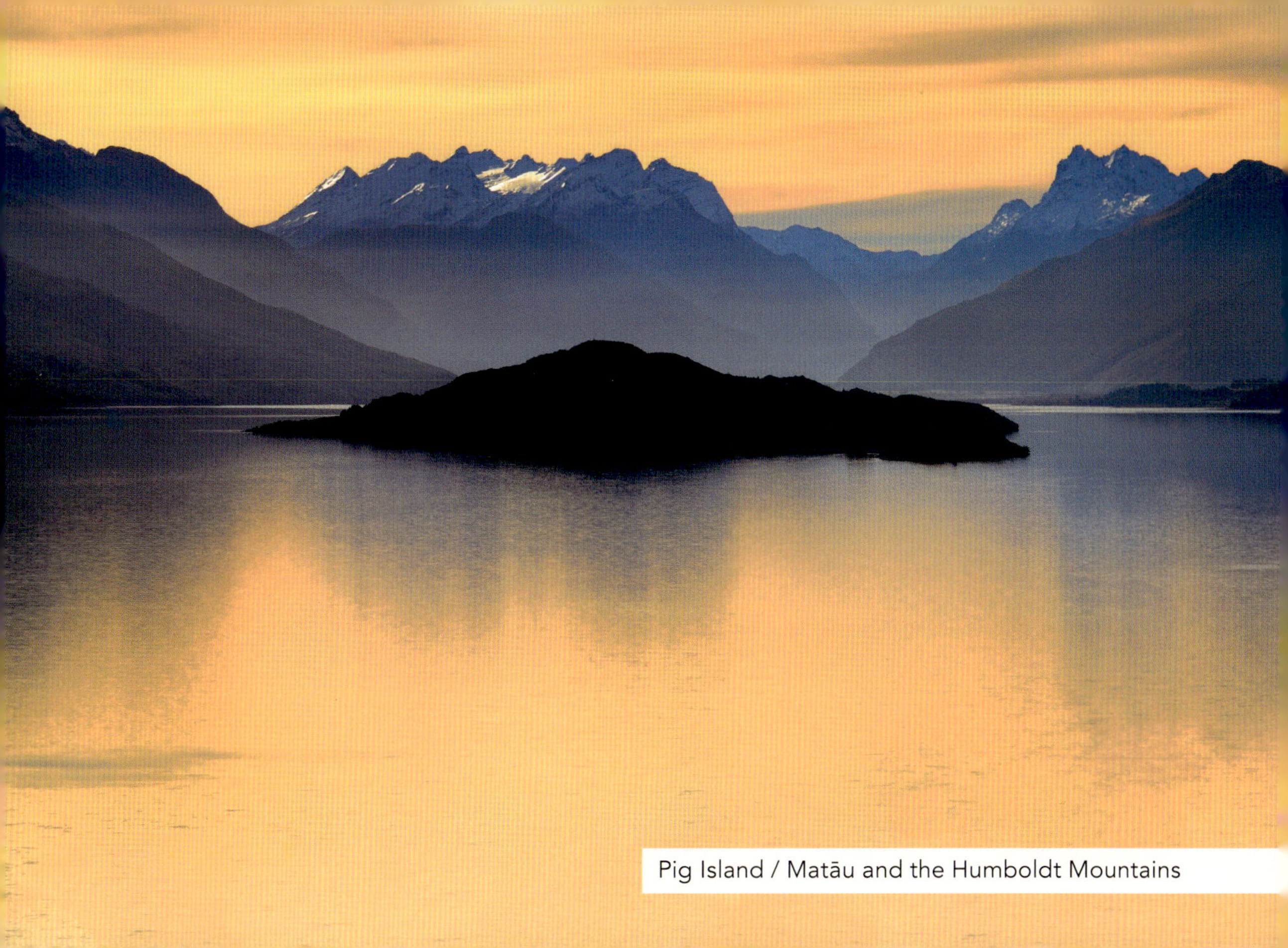

Pig Island / Matāu and the Humboldt Mountains

Glenorchy

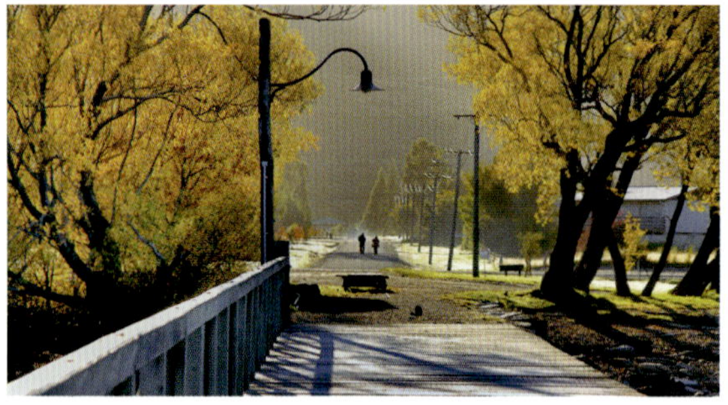

Morning stroll, Islay Street

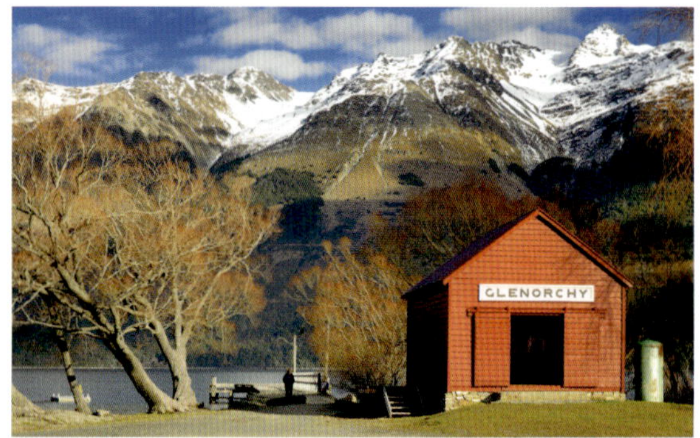

Iconic red shed on Glenorchy wharf

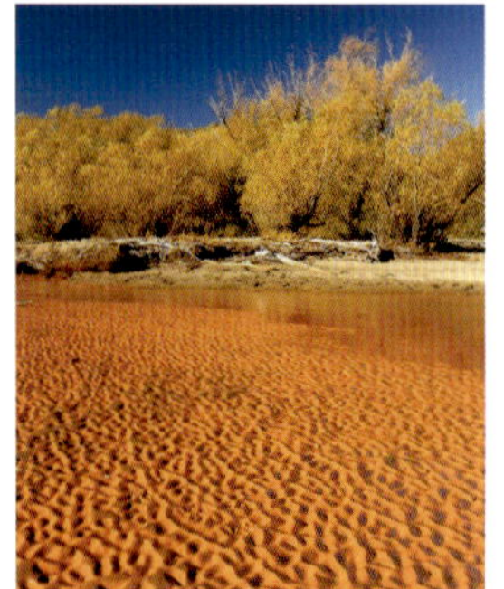

Lake edge alluvial sediment

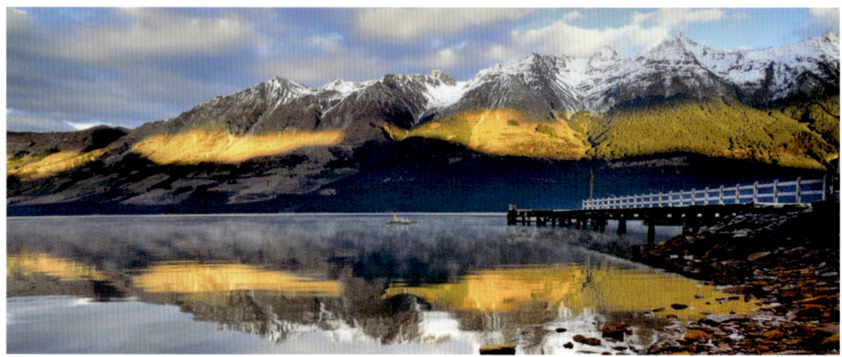

Humboldt Mountain Range

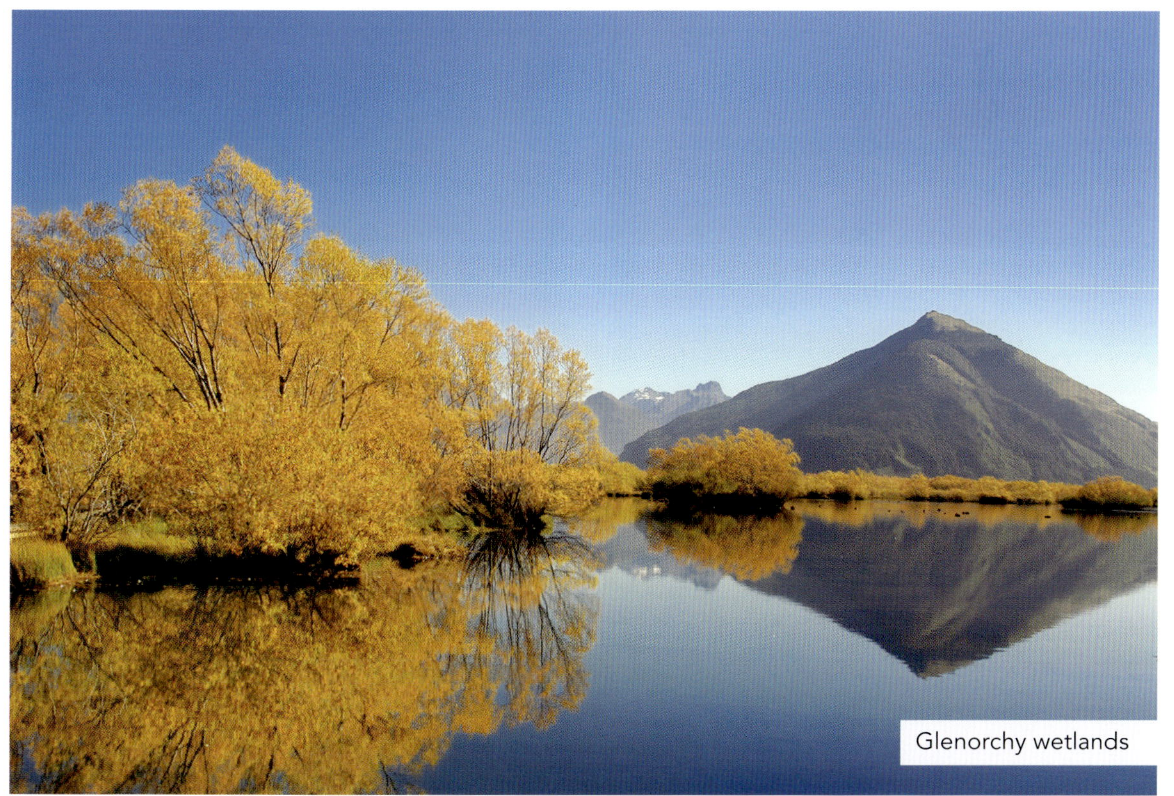
Glenorchy wetlands

12

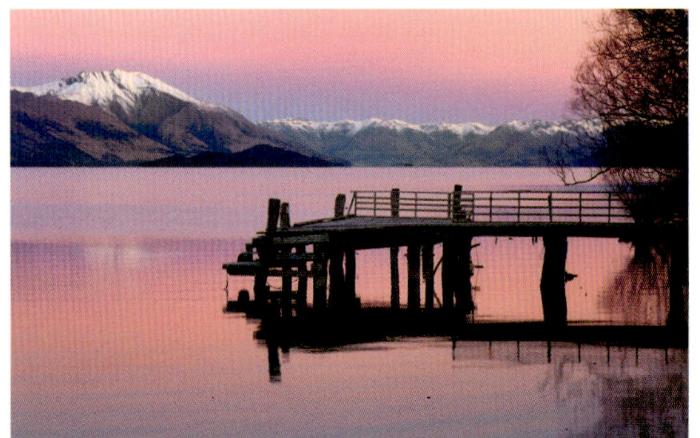
Evening, Kinloch

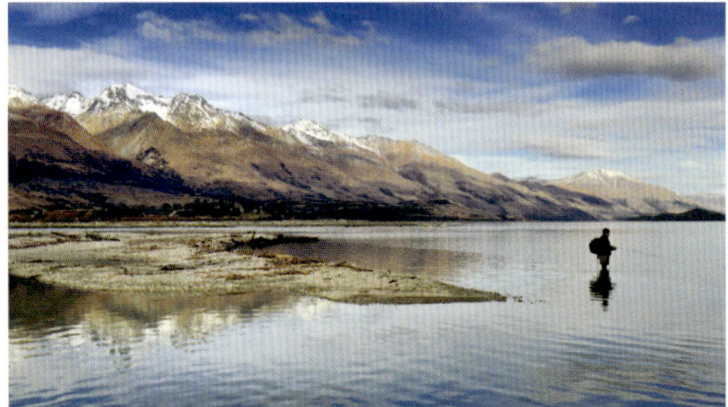
Trout fishing, Kinloch

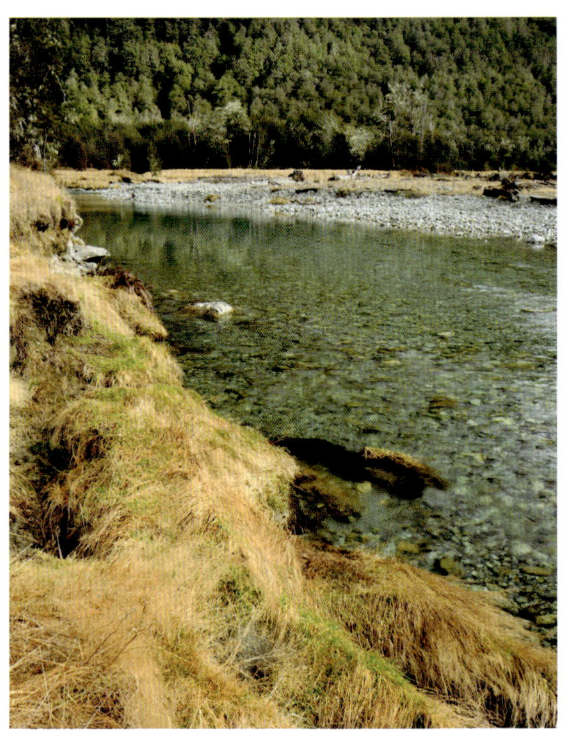
The start of the Routeburn Track

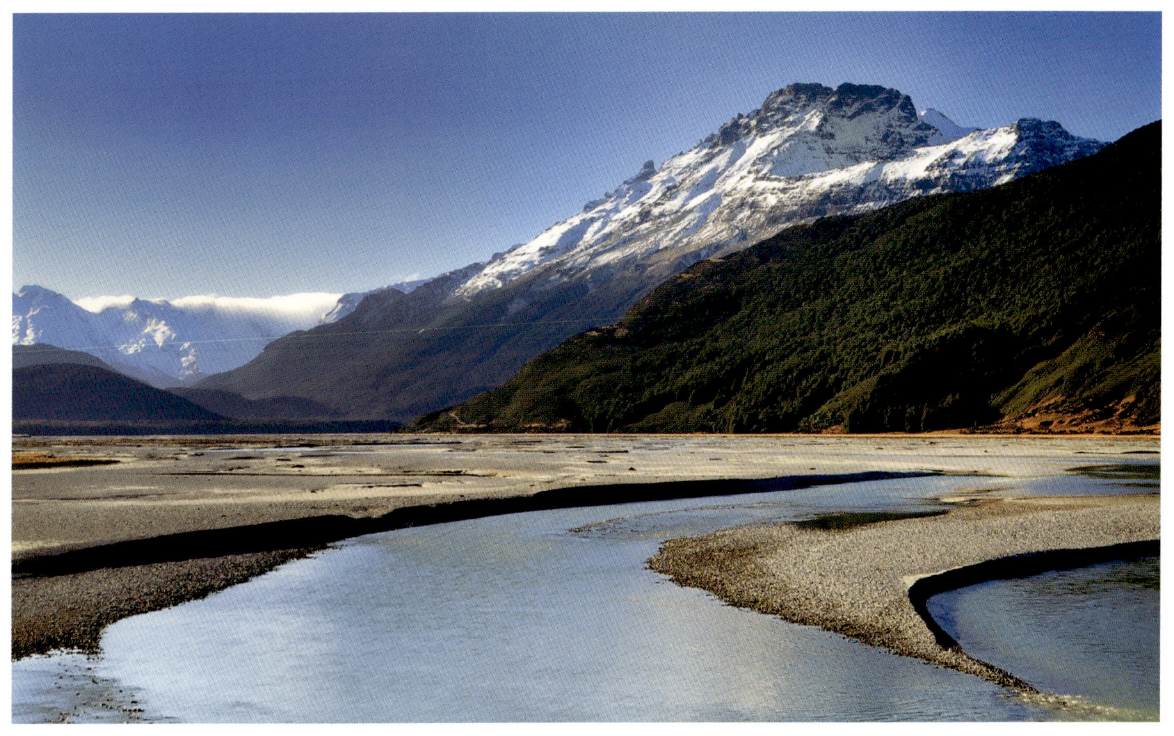

Dart River / Te Awa Wakatipu, northern end of Lake Wakatipu, near Glenorchy

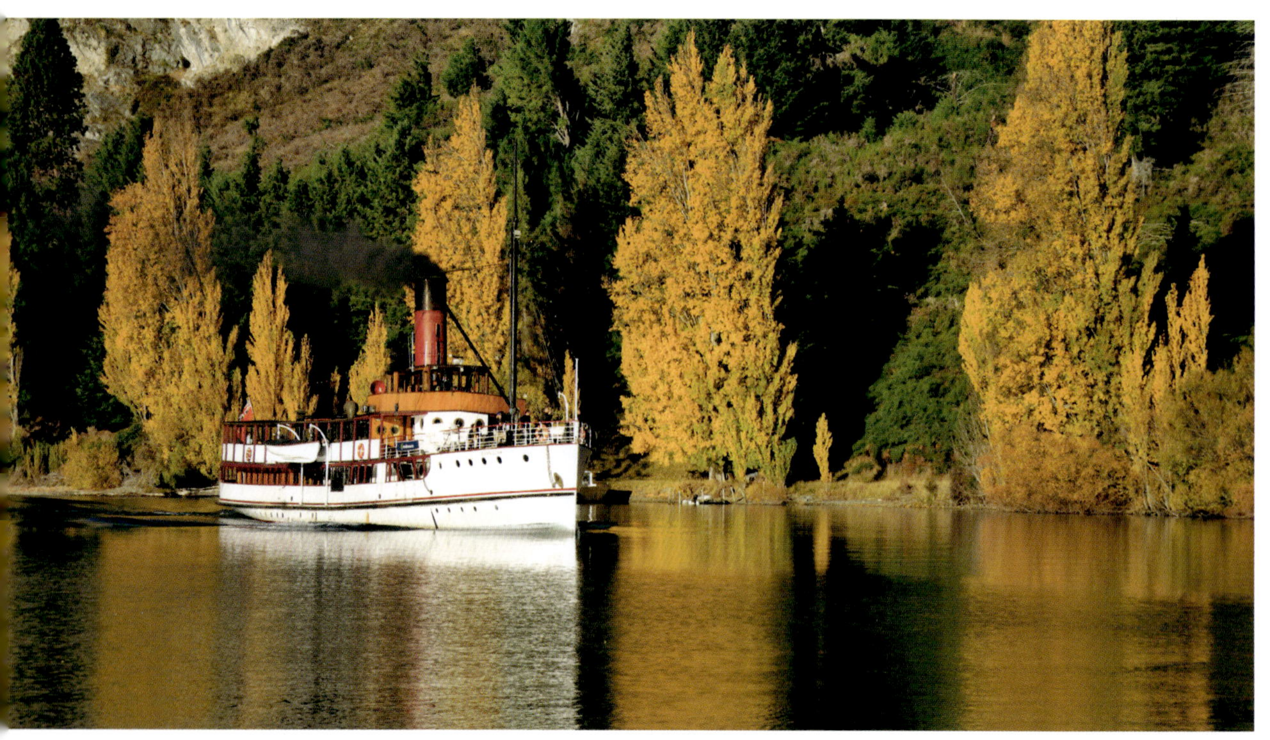

SS *Earnslaw* approaching Walter Peak Station

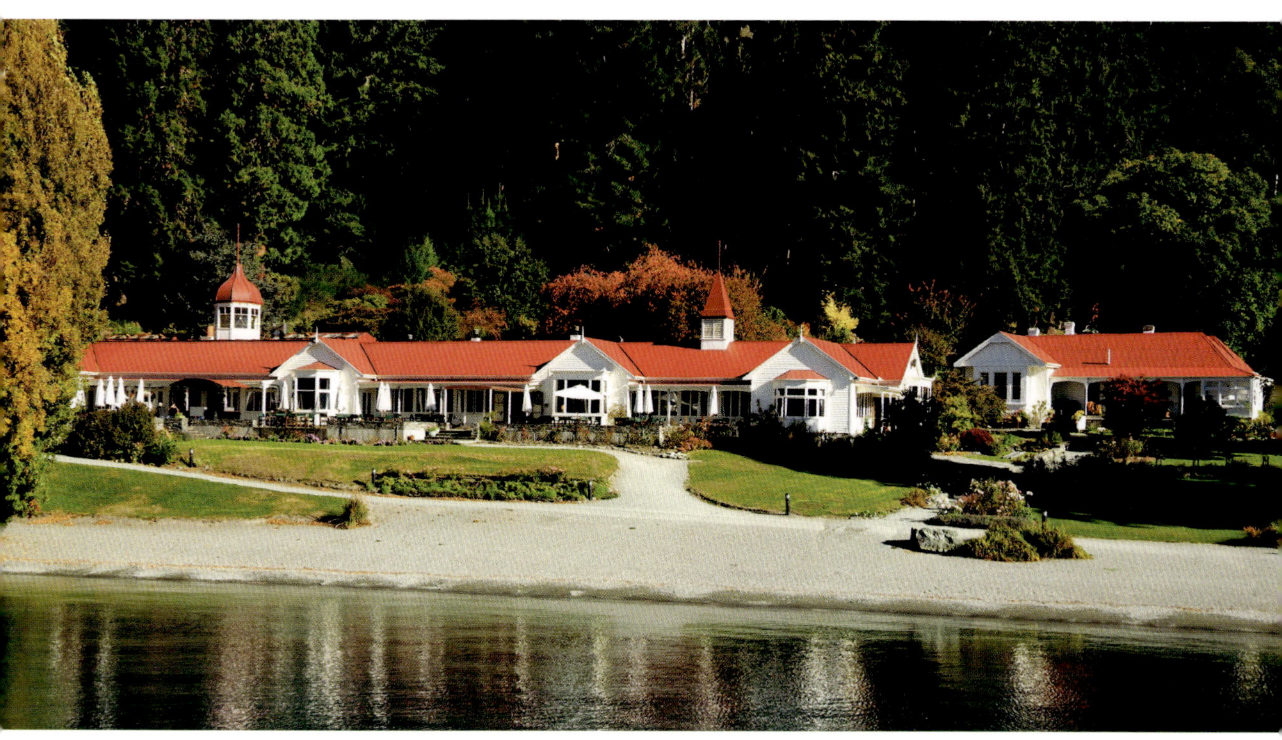

Walter Peak Station

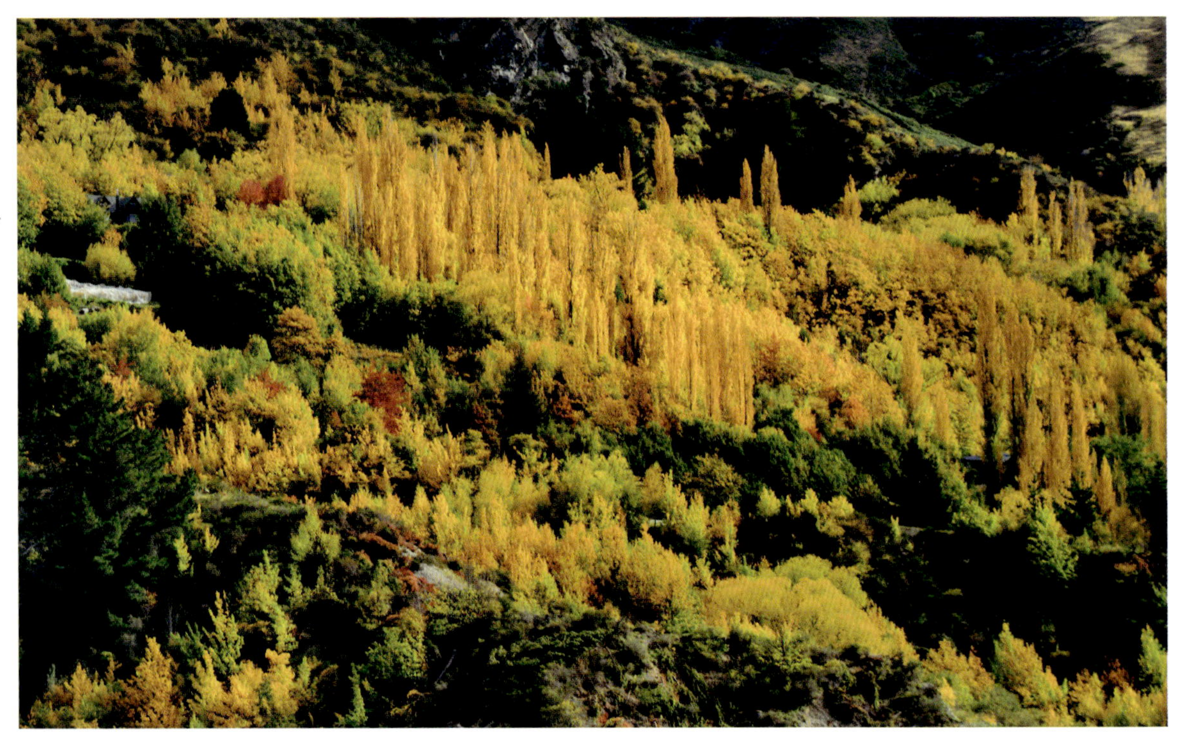

Arthurs Point

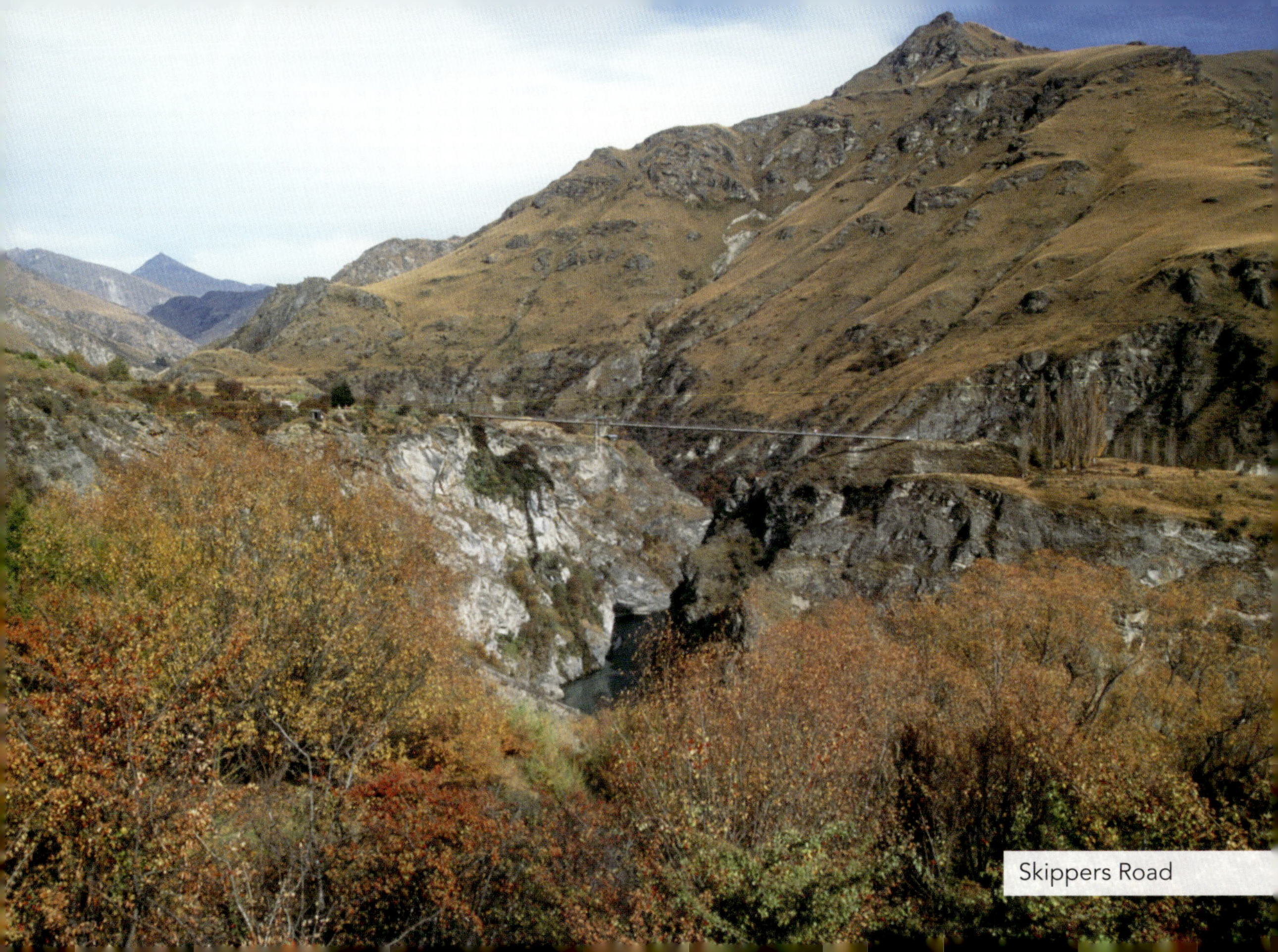

Skippers Road

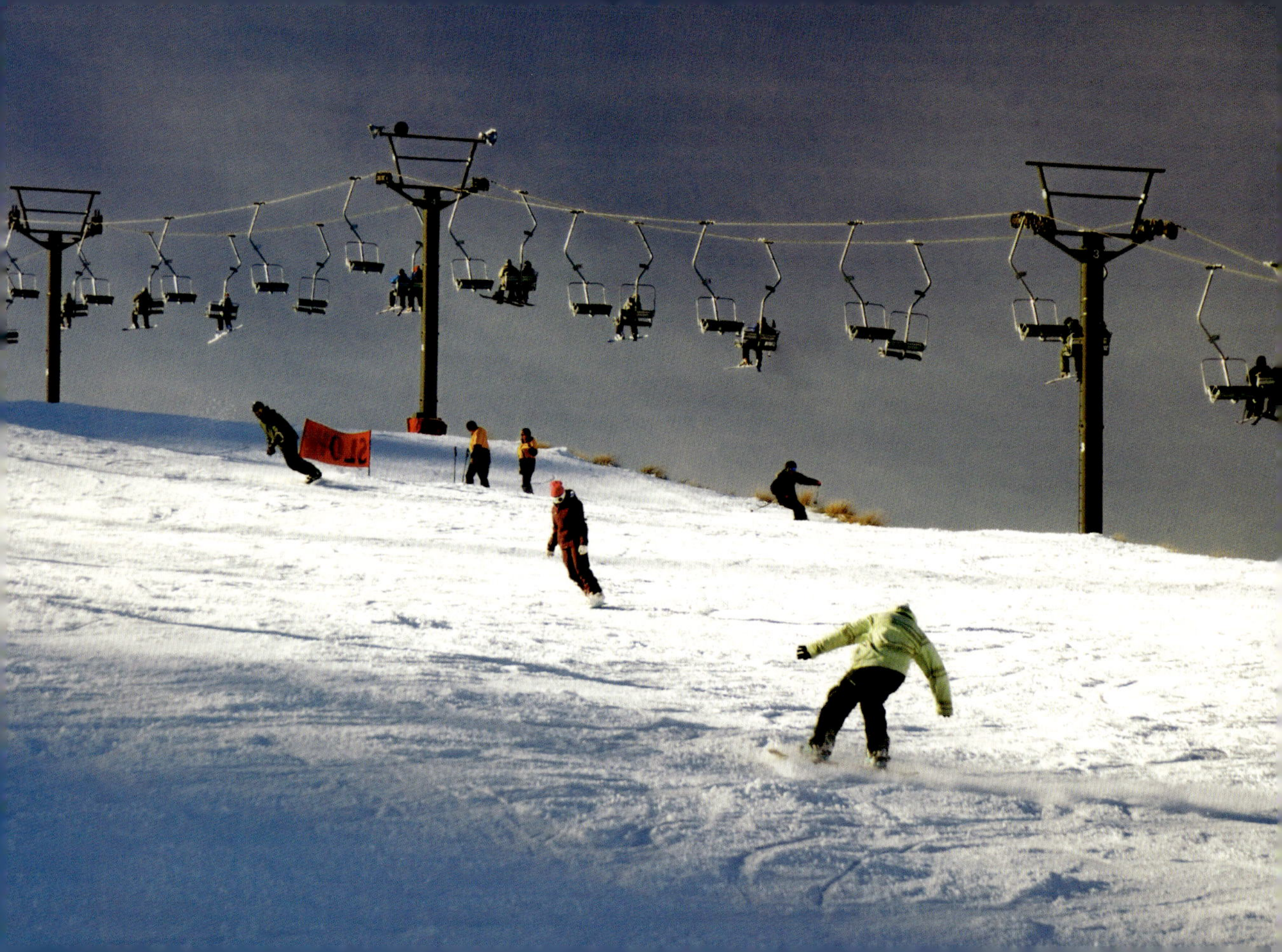

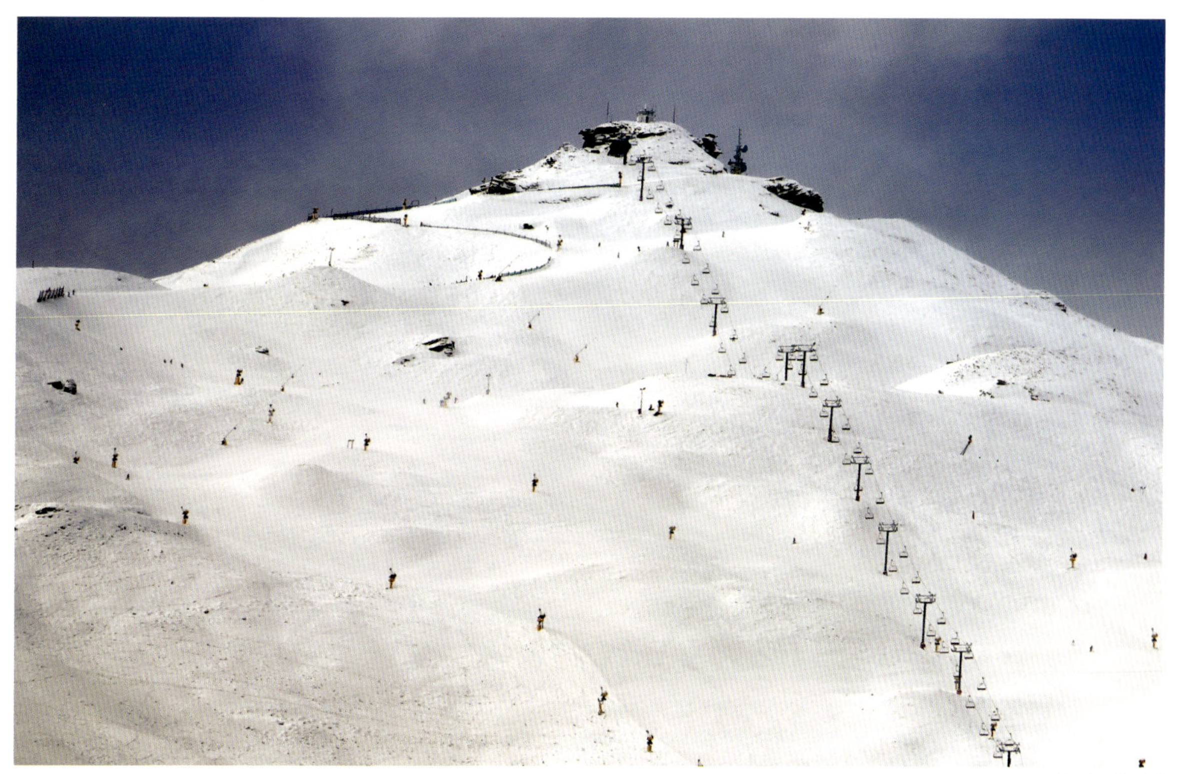

Coronet Peak ski field

Arrowtown

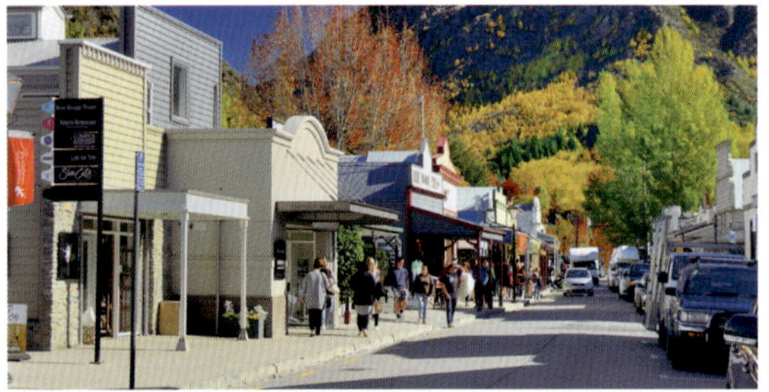

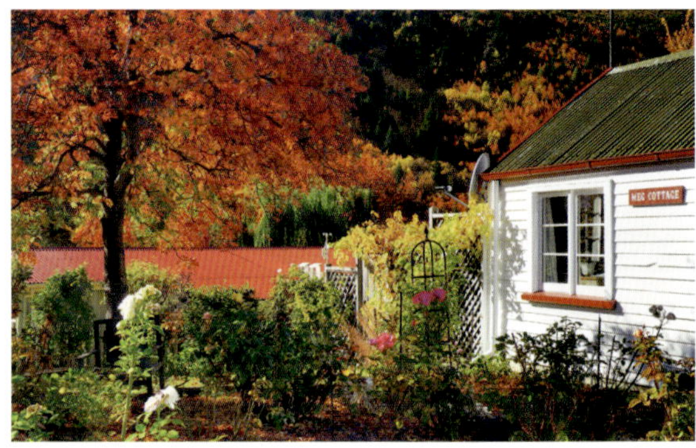

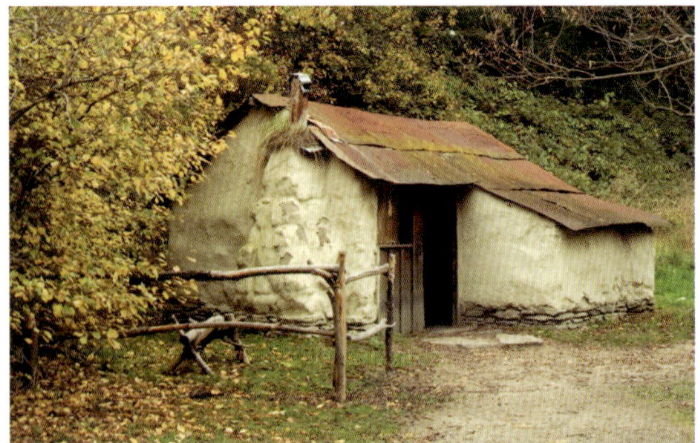

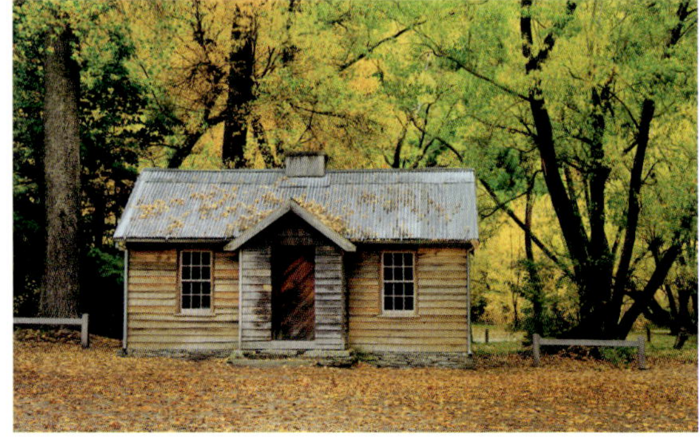

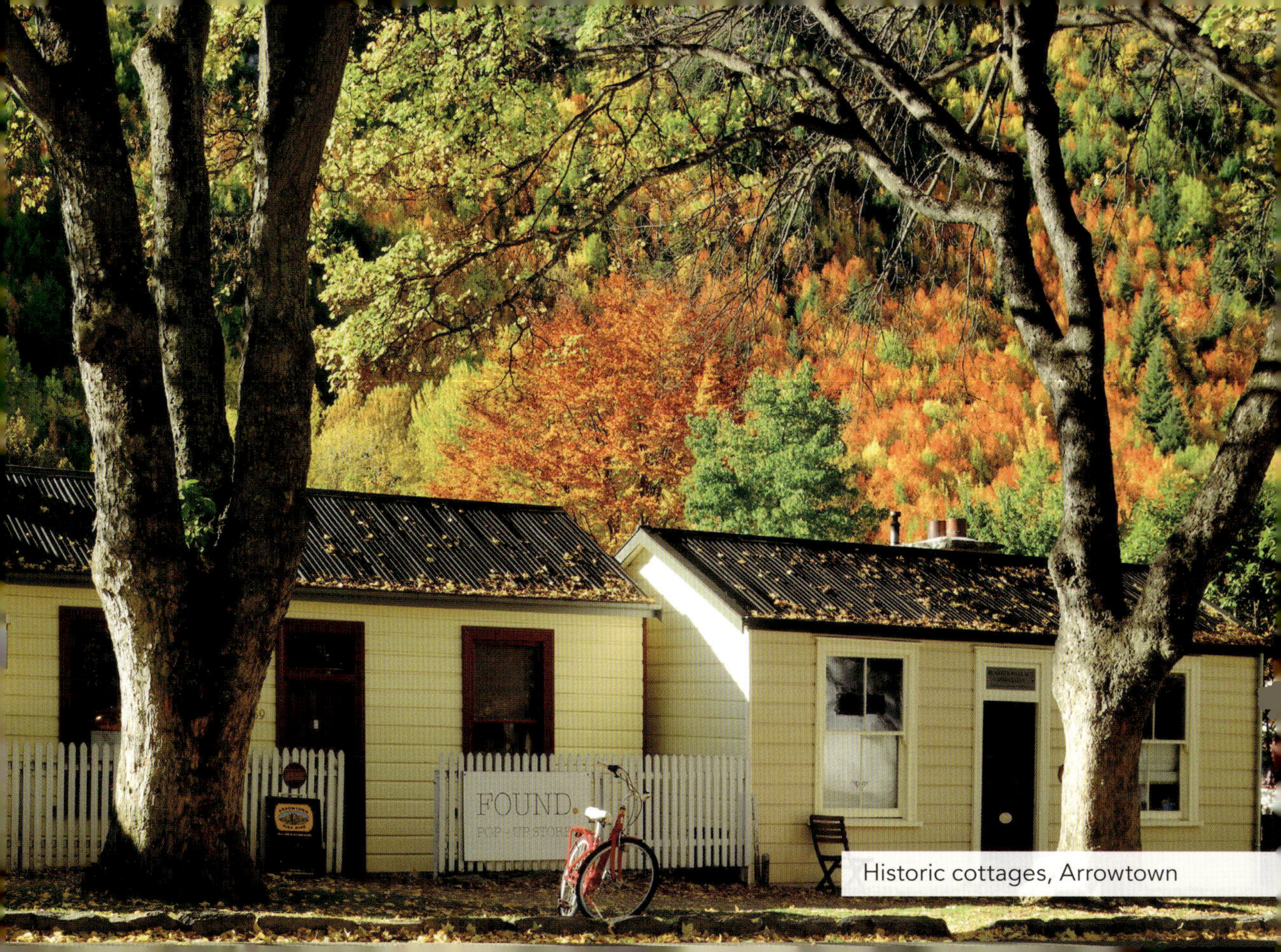

Historic cottages, Arrowtown

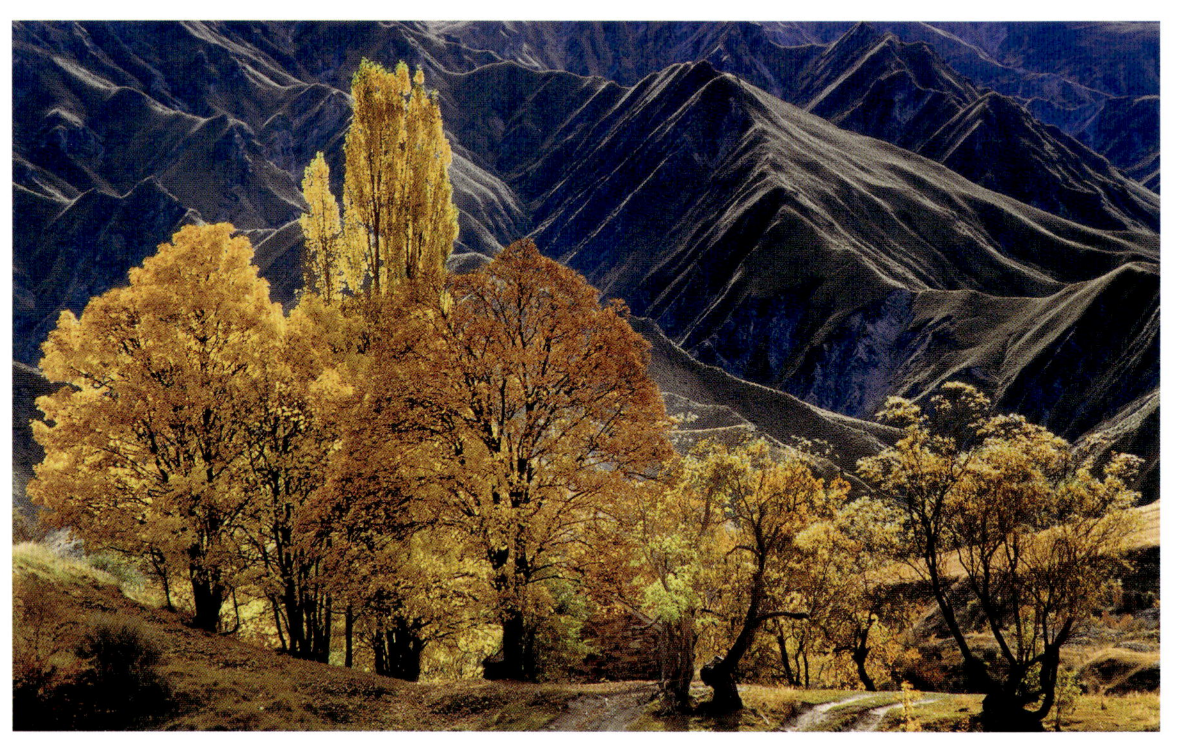

Macetown

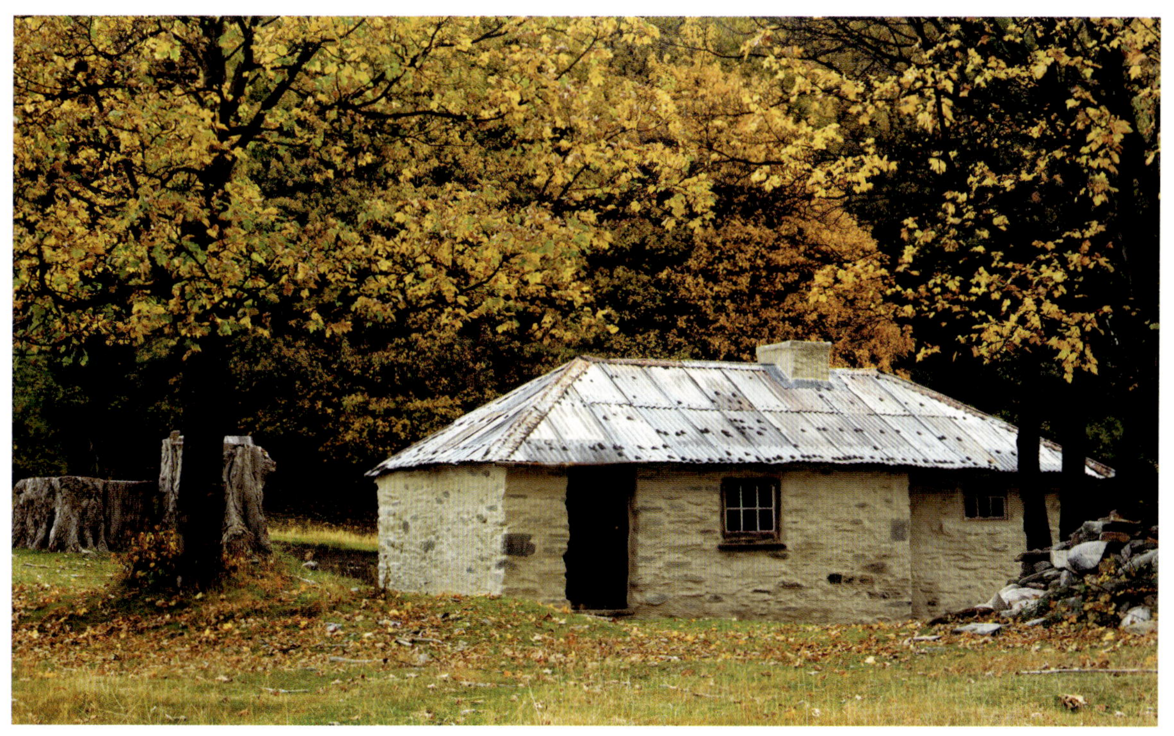

Abandoned stone cottage, Macetown

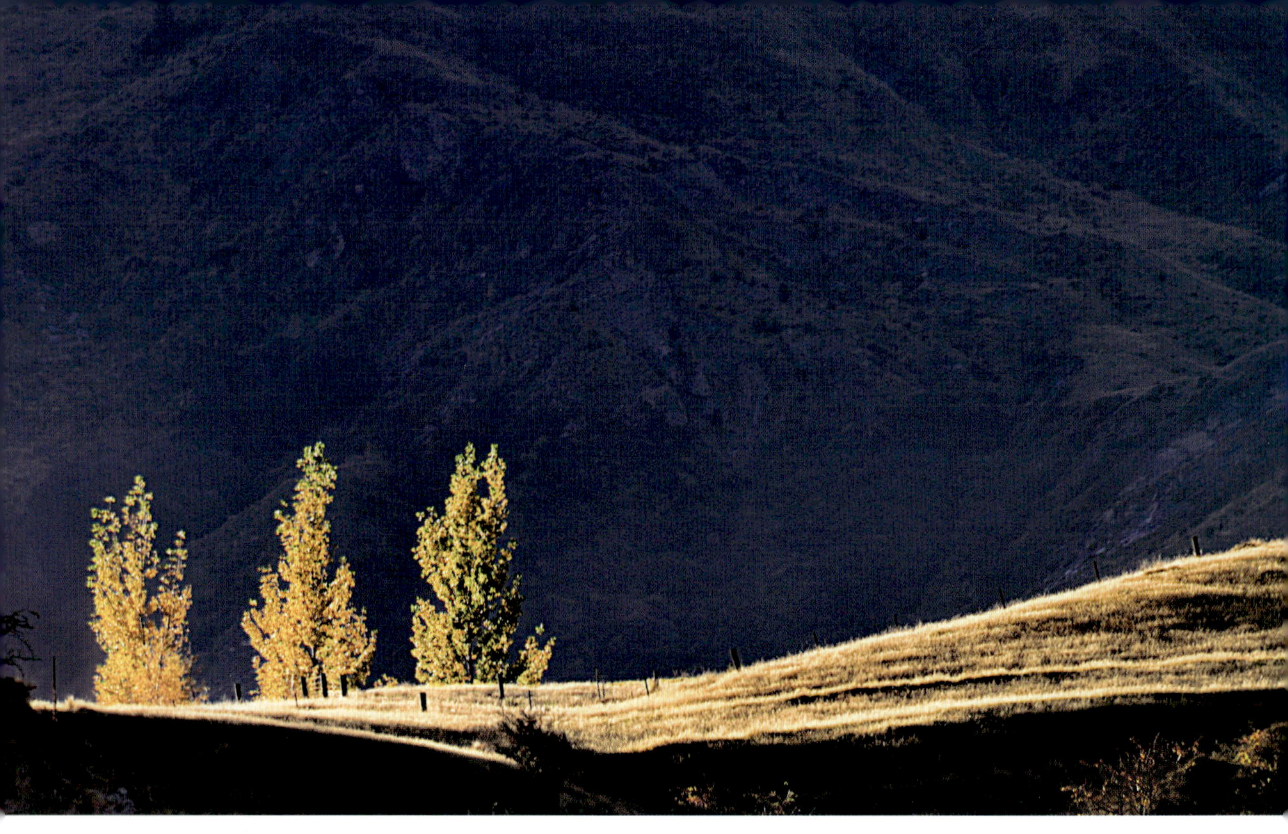

Speargrass Flat

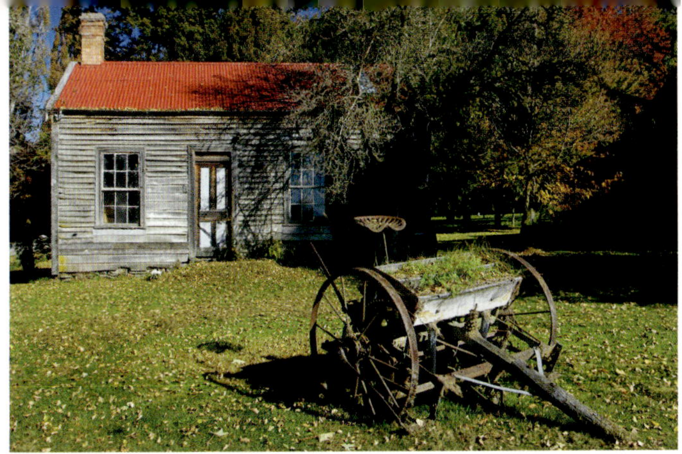

Speargrass Flat (above and below)

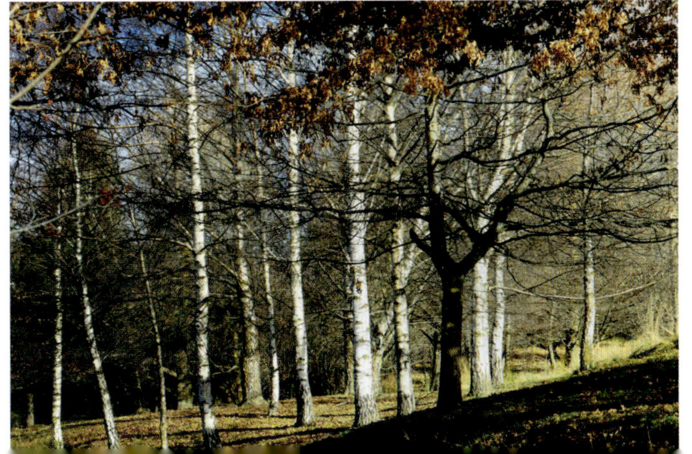

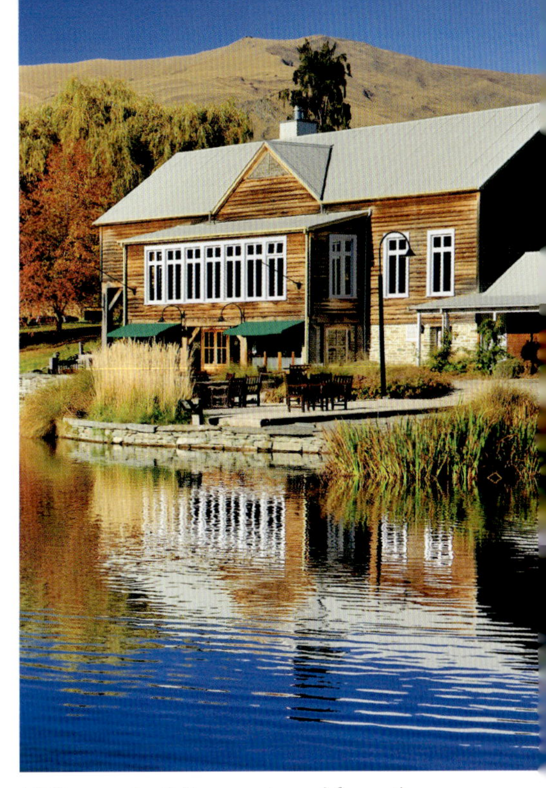

Millhouse building, restored from the original wheat mill, Millbrook Resort

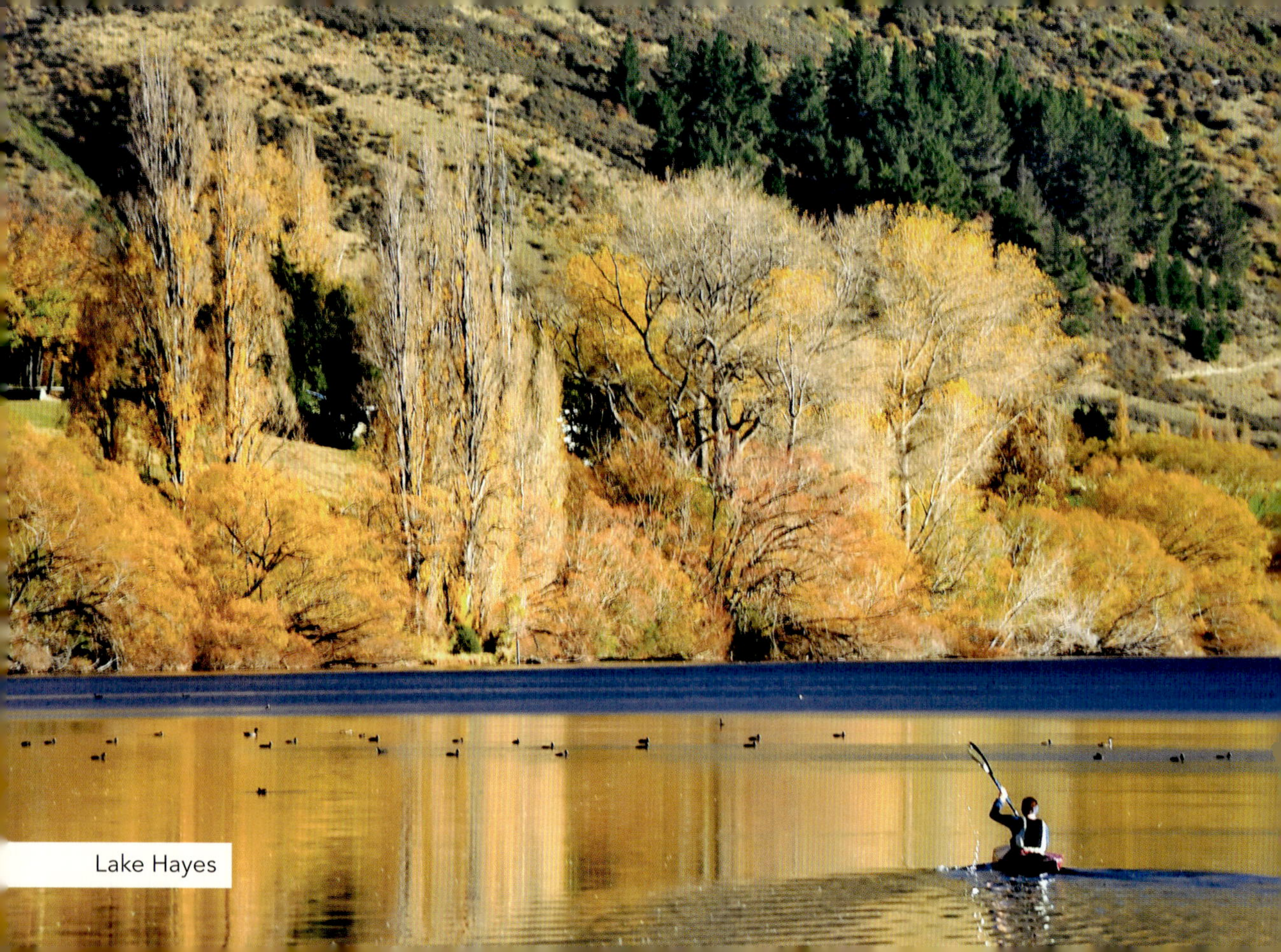
Lake Hayes

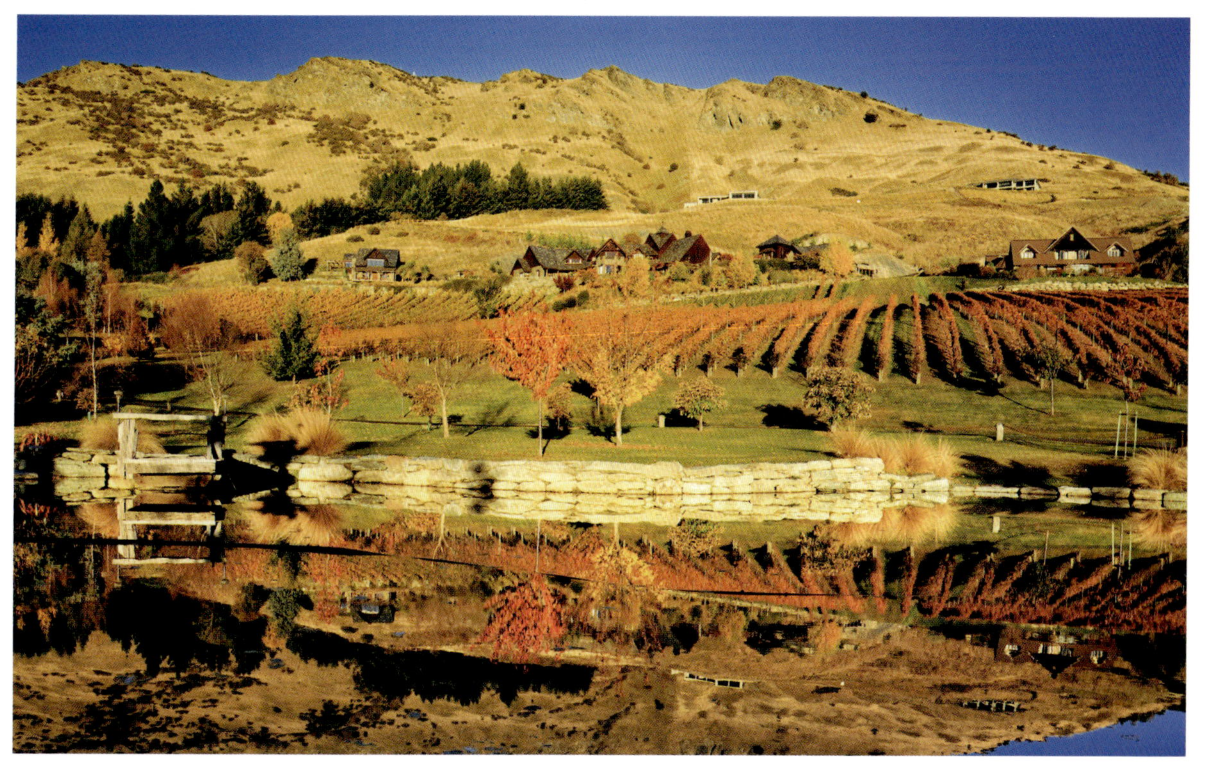

Vineyard near Lake Hayes

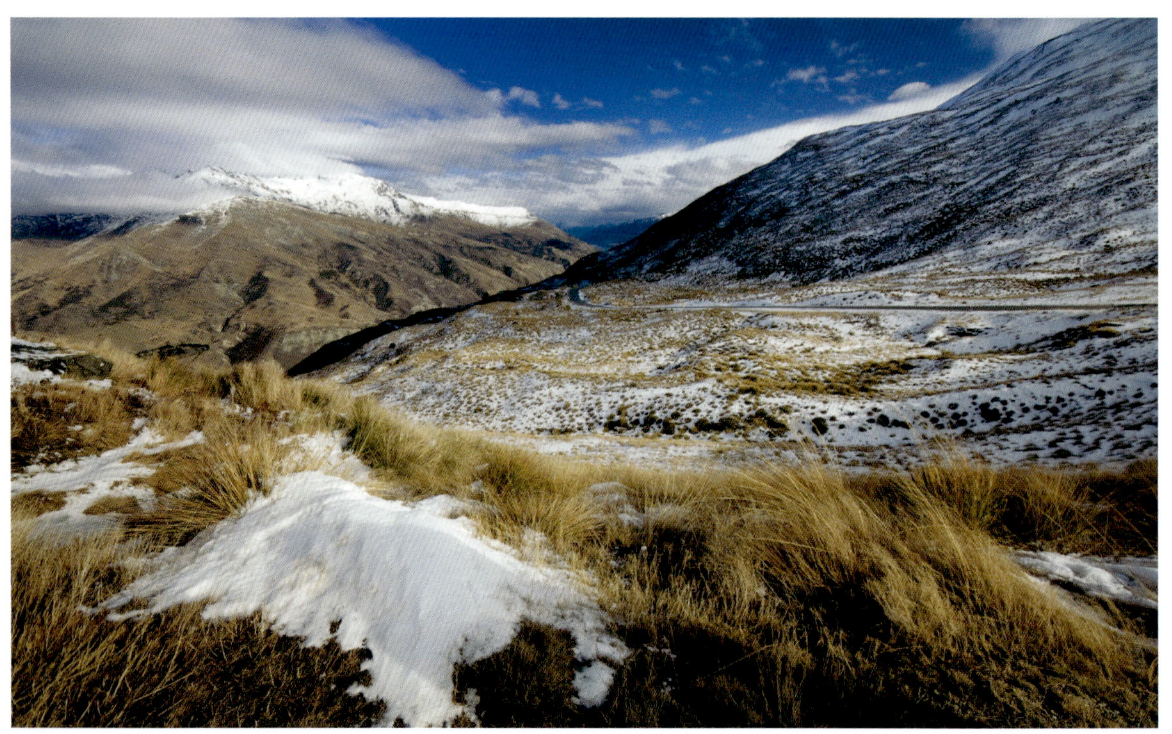

Summit of the Crown Range

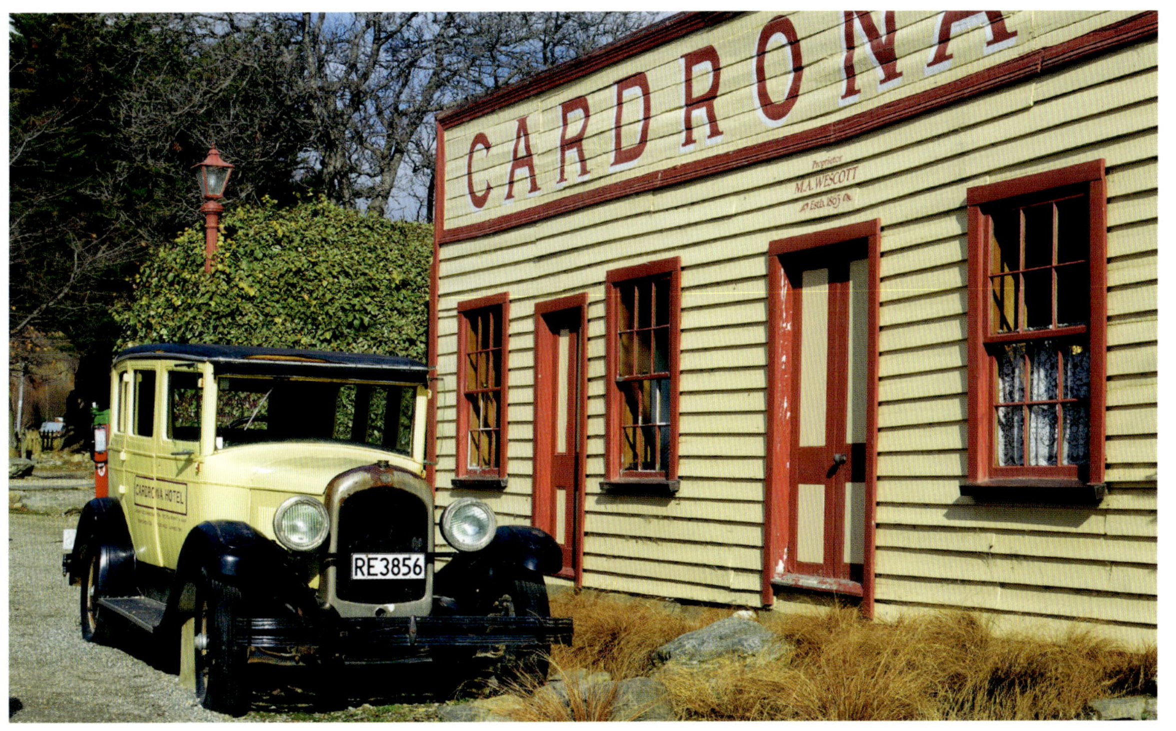

Cardrona Hotel on the Crown Range Road

Wānaka

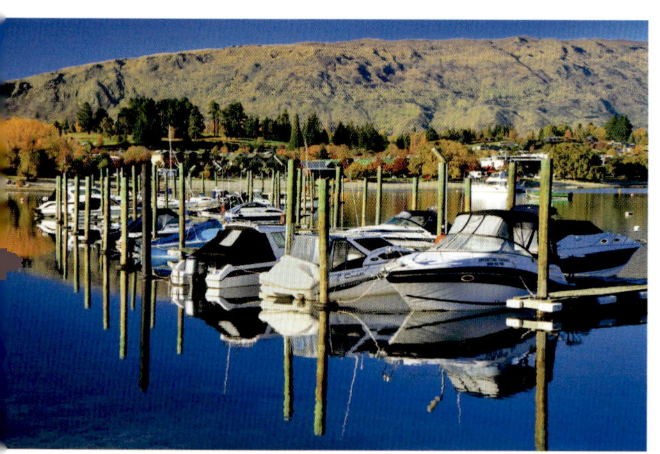

Marina, Wānaka township

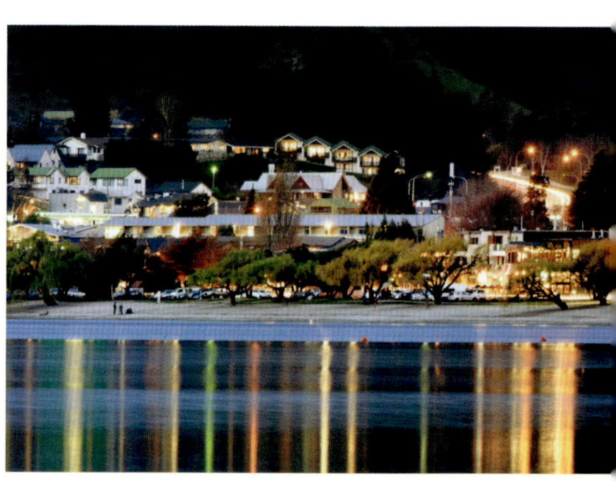

Wānaka township

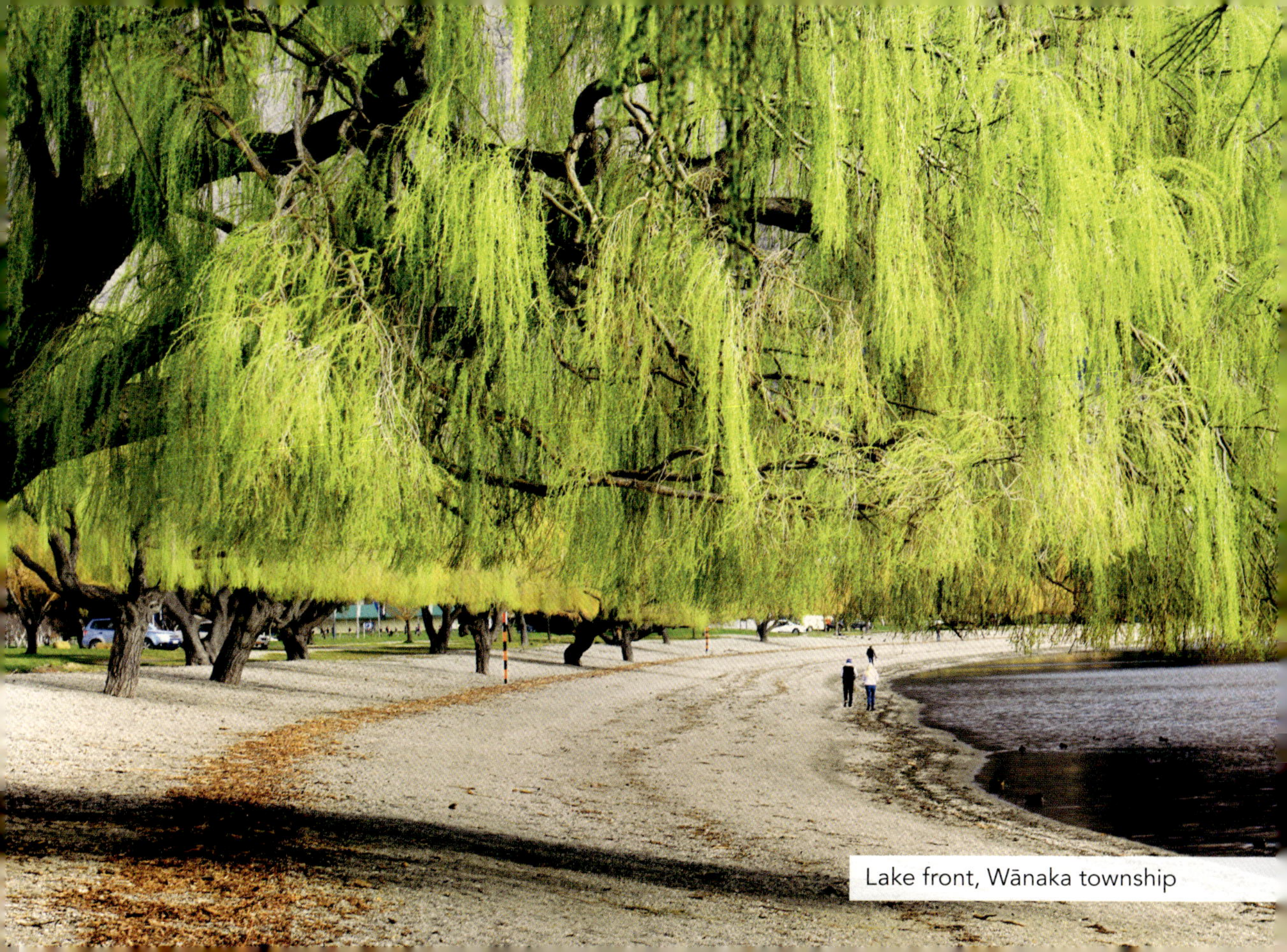
Lake front, Wānaka township

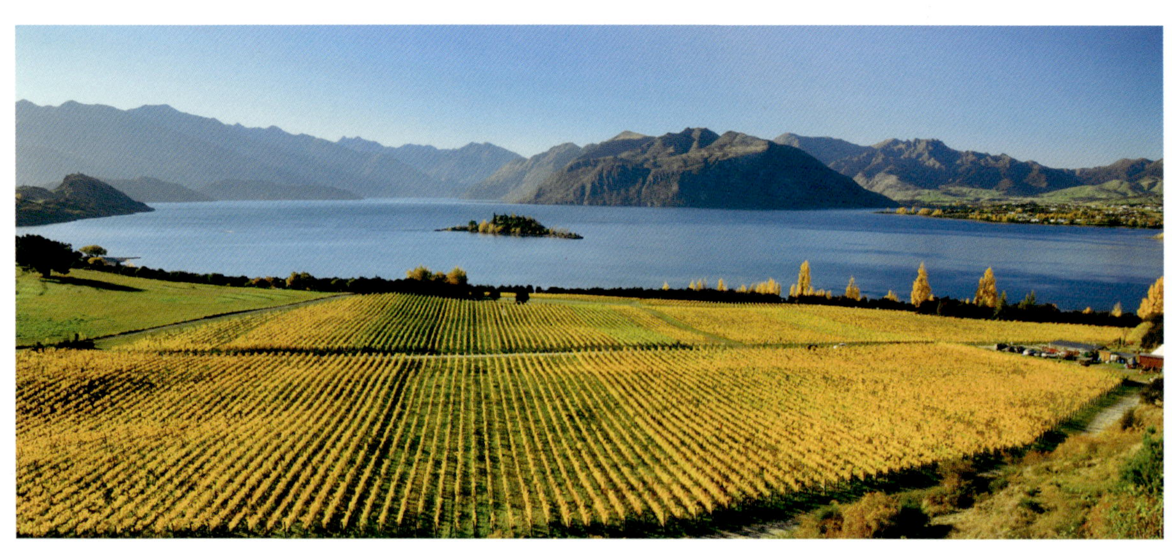

Rippon Vineyard, Lake Wānaka

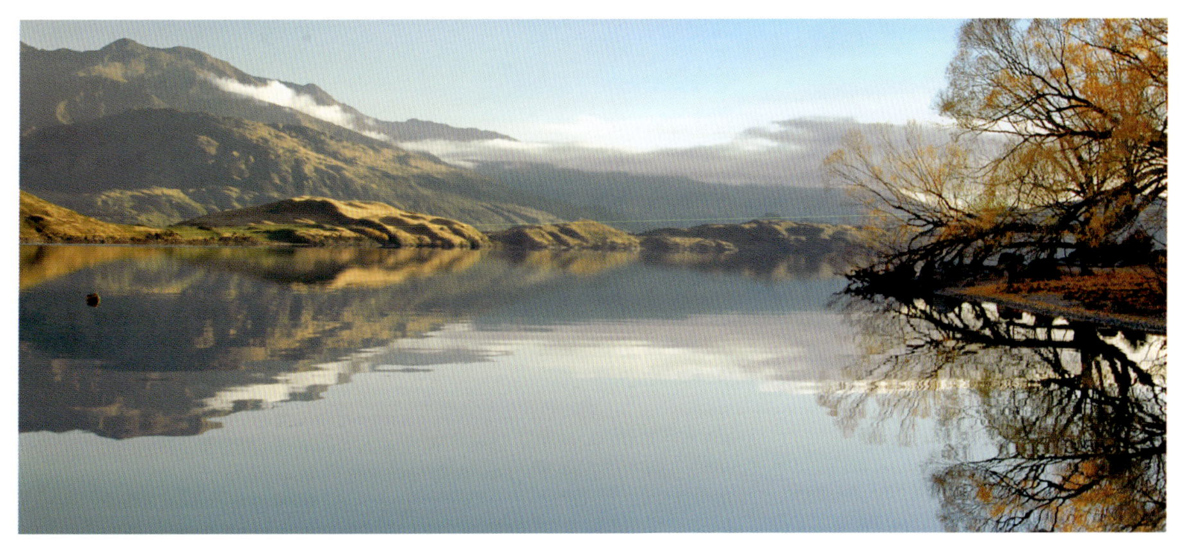

Glendhu Bay, Lake Wānaka

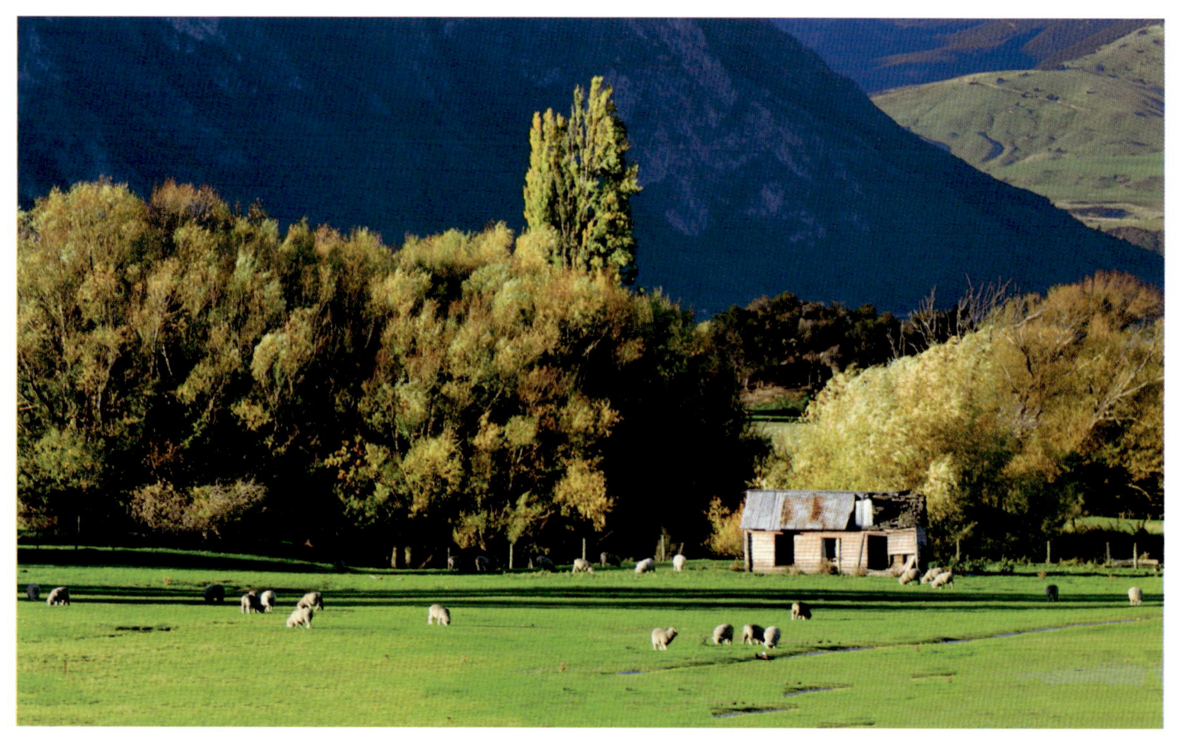

Countryside, Wānaka Mount Aspiring Road

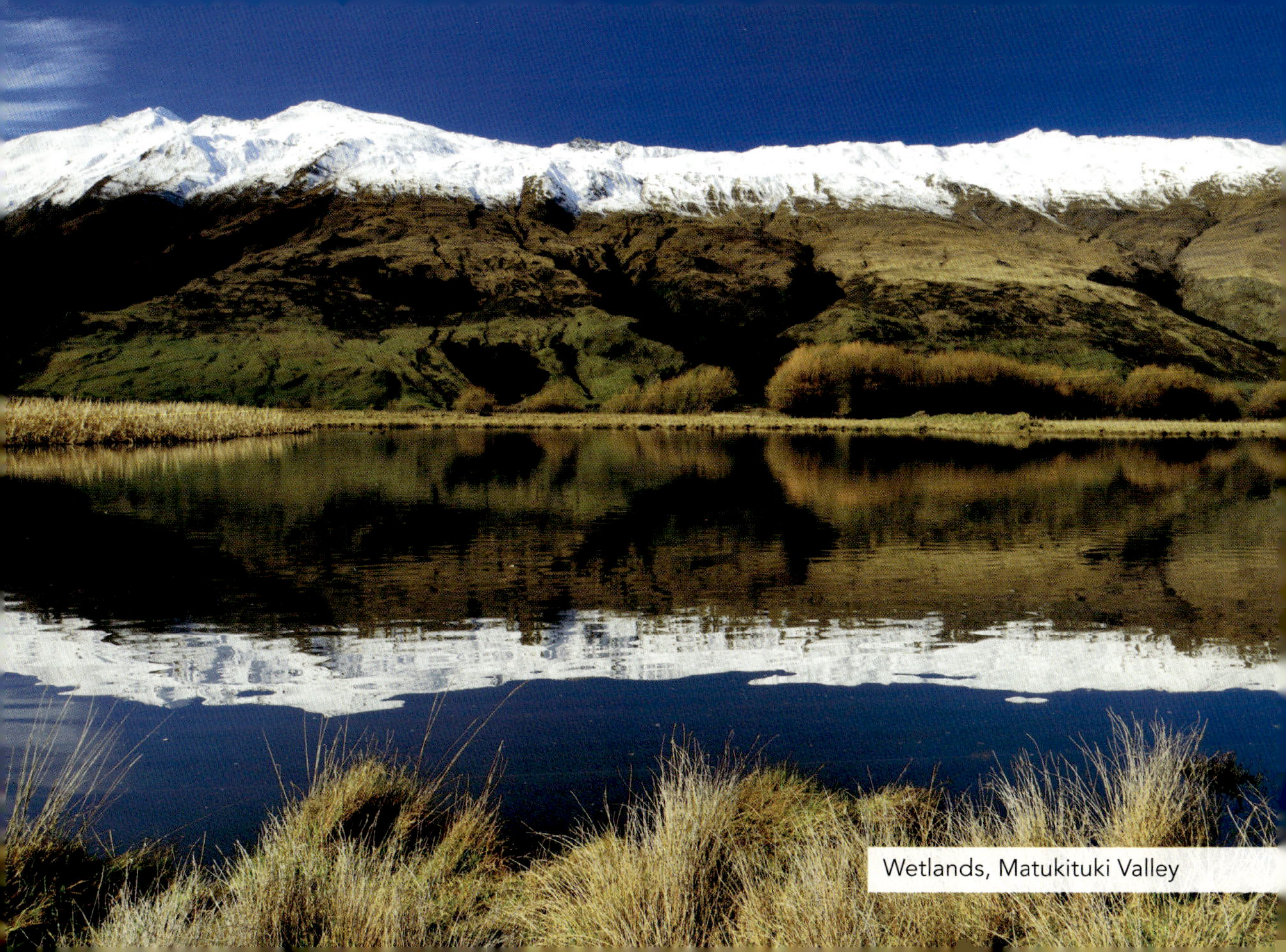

Wetlands, Matukituki Valley

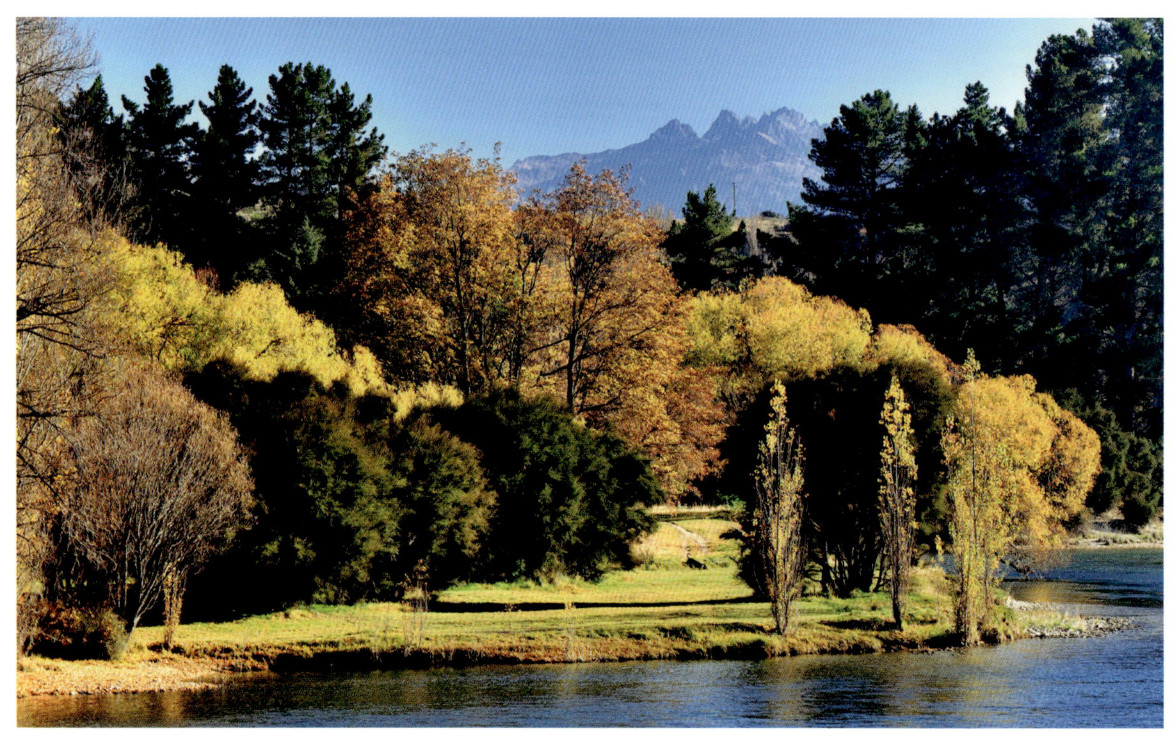

Clutha River / Mata-Au, Albert Town

From Hāwea to Haast

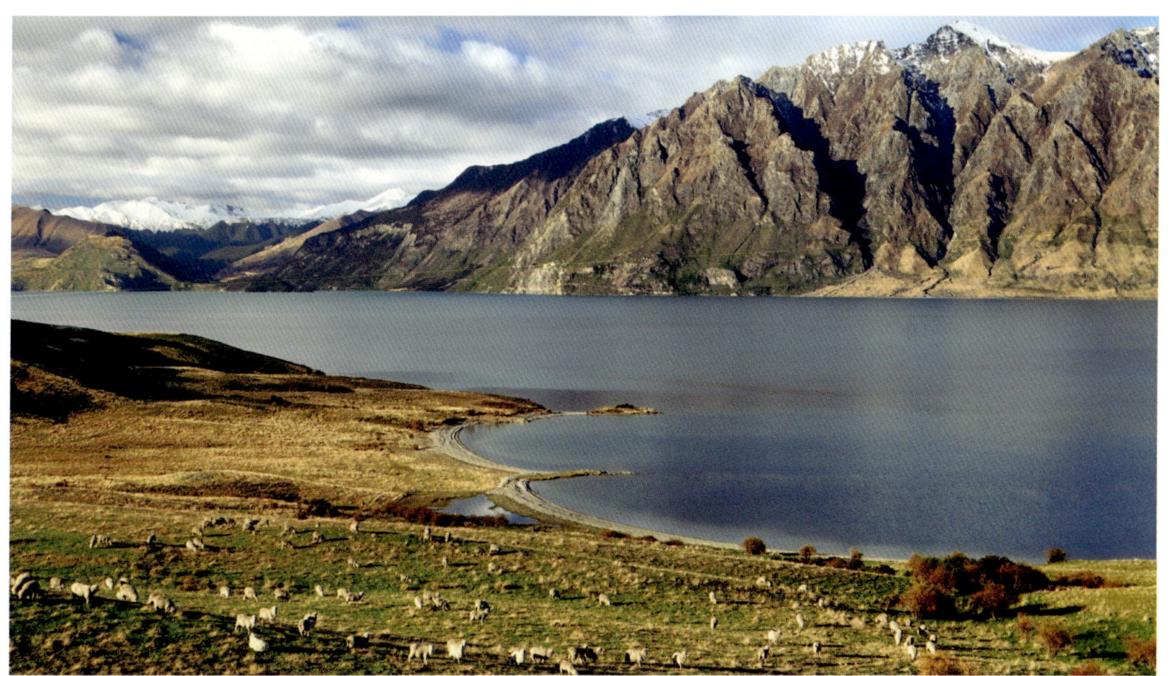

Countryside beside Lake Hāwea

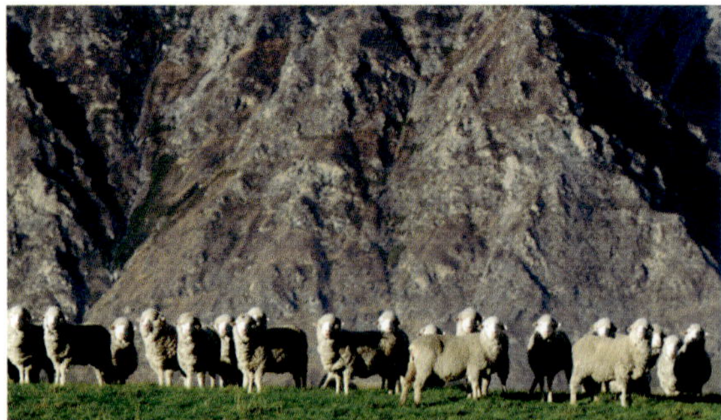

38 Sheep near Lake Hāwea

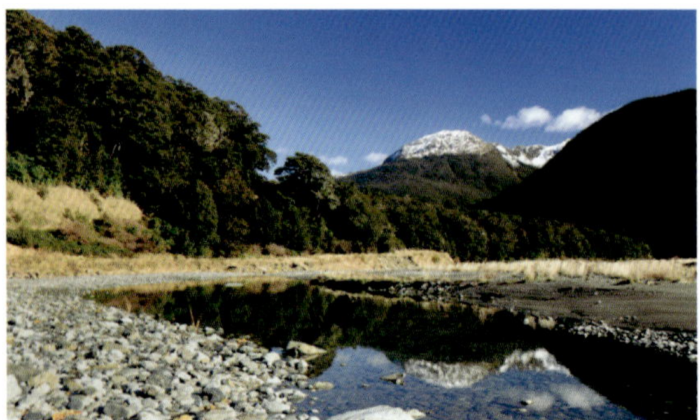

Makarora River, Haast Pass Highway

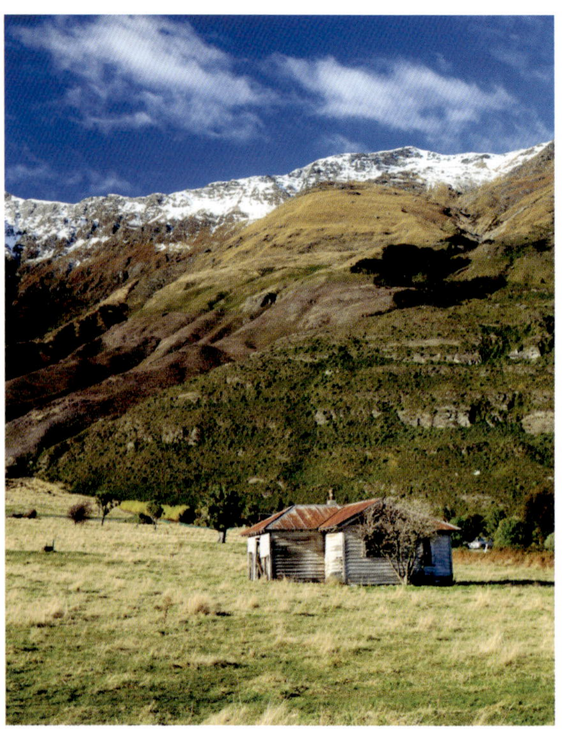

Abandoned homestead, Makarora

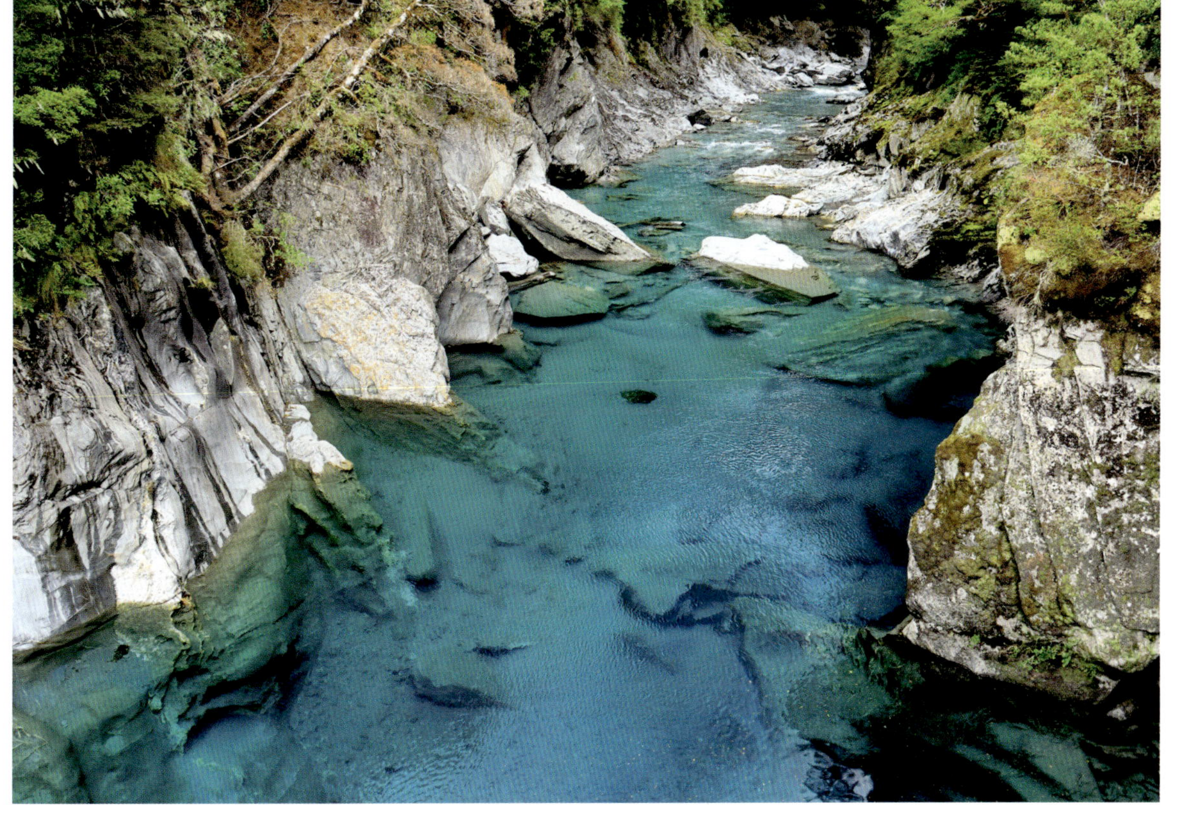

Blue River and Blue Pools, Makarora Valley

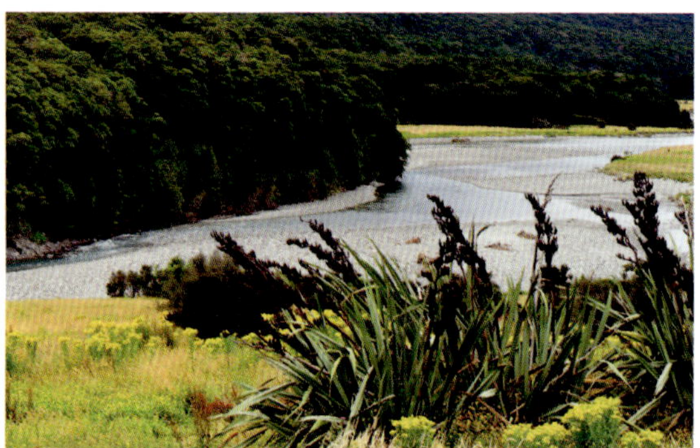

Cameron Flat and the Makarora River

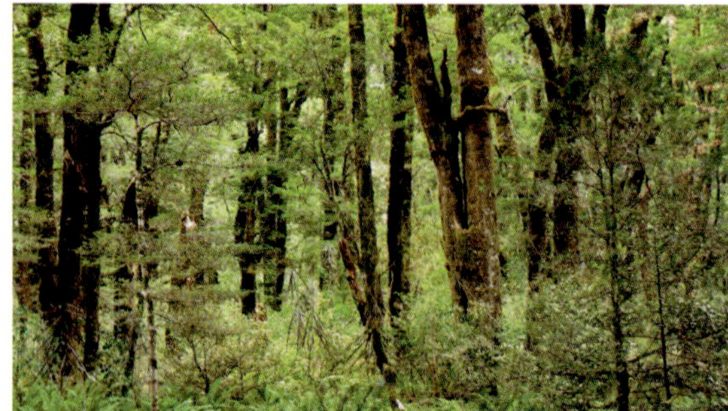

Beech forest, Makarora Valley

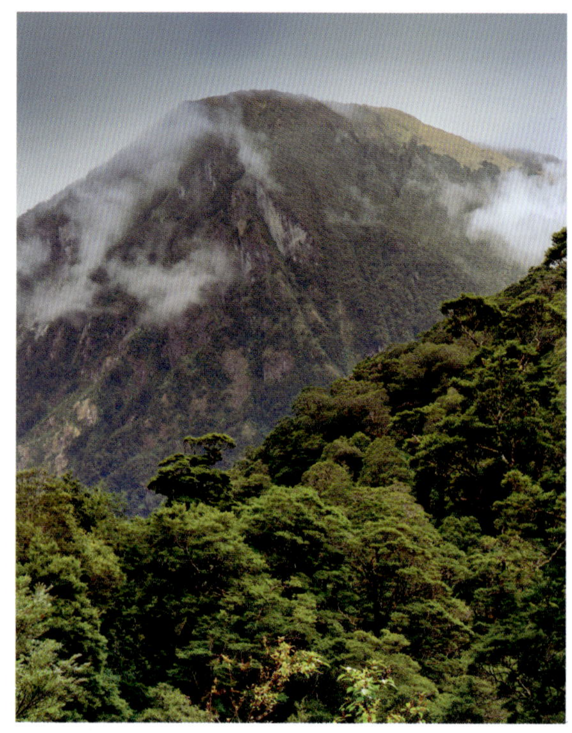

Summit of the Haast Pass / Tīoripātea Highway

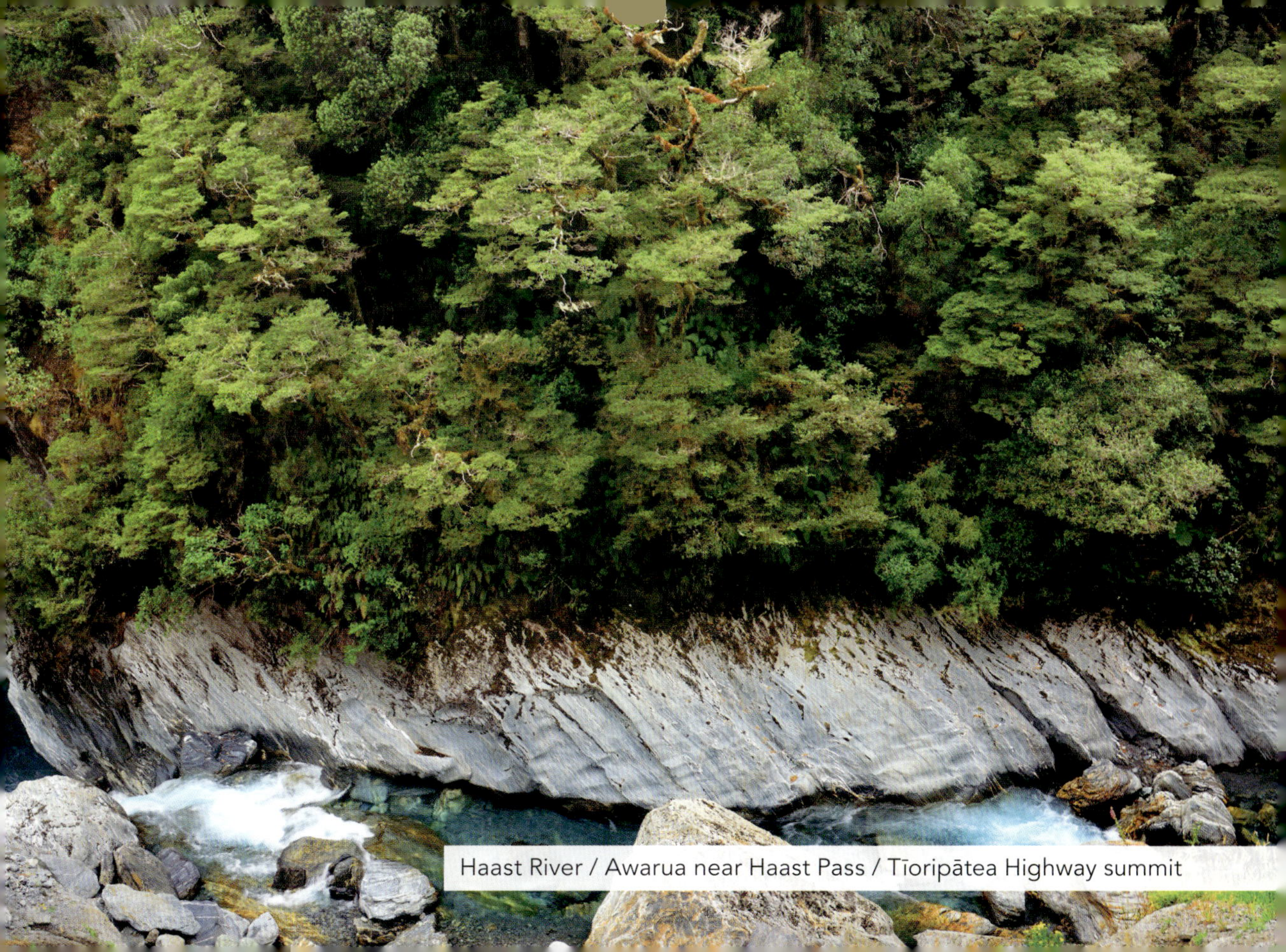

Haast River / Awarua near Haast Pass / Tīoripātea Highway summit

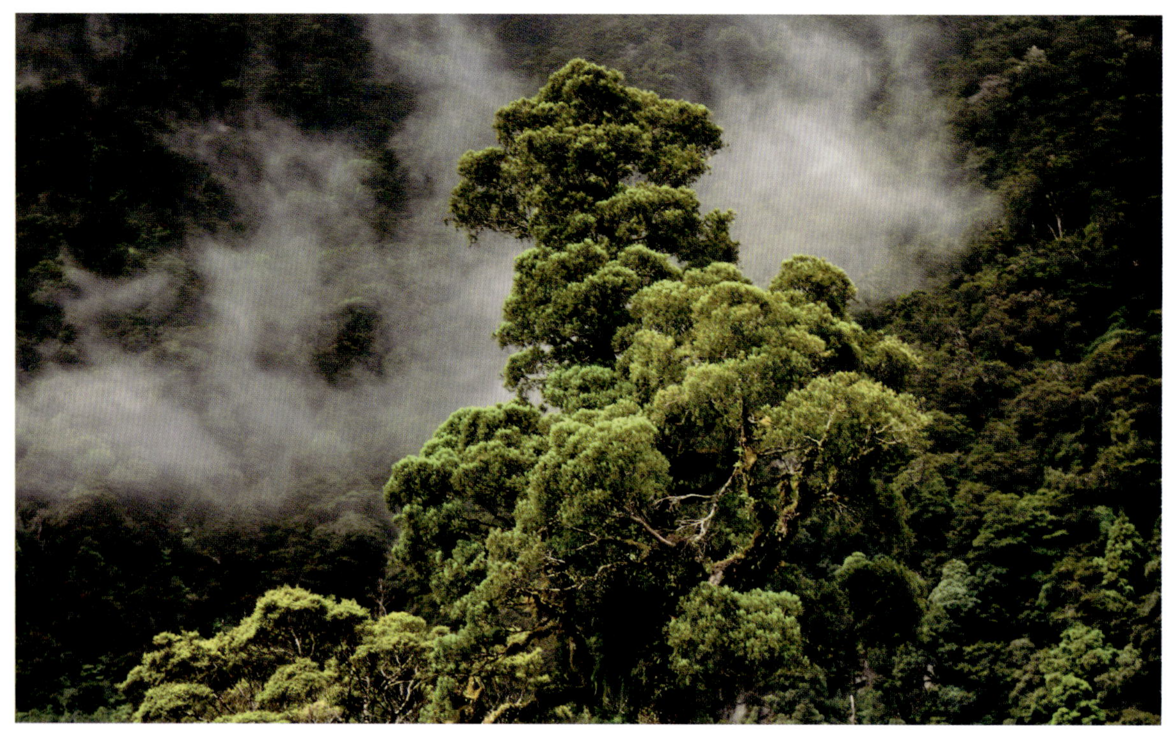

Rainforest, Haast Pass / Tīoripātea Highway

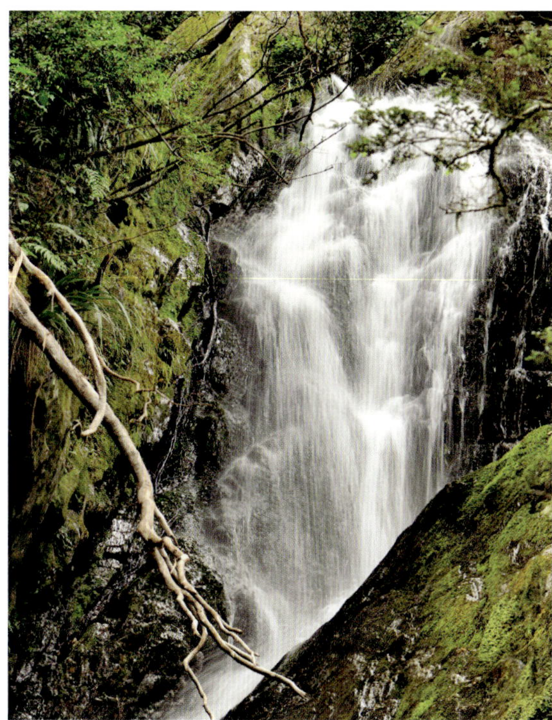

The Trickle No.2, Haast Pass / Tīoripātea Highway

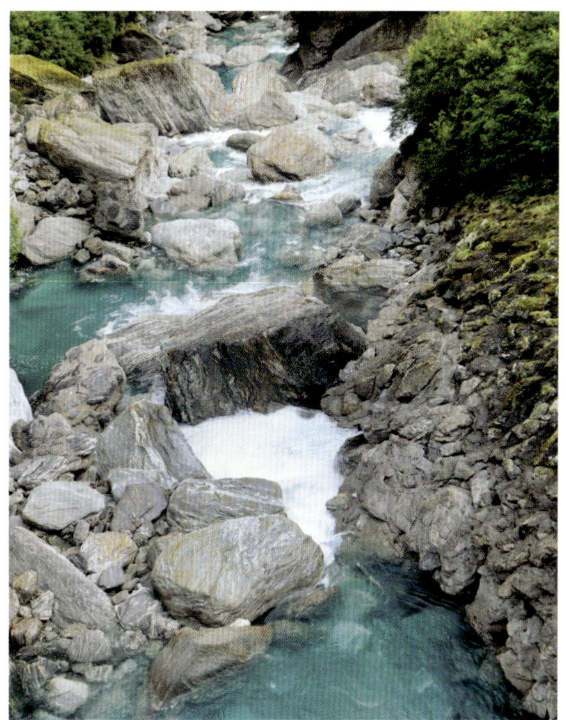

Gates of Haast, Haast Pass / Tīoripātea Highway

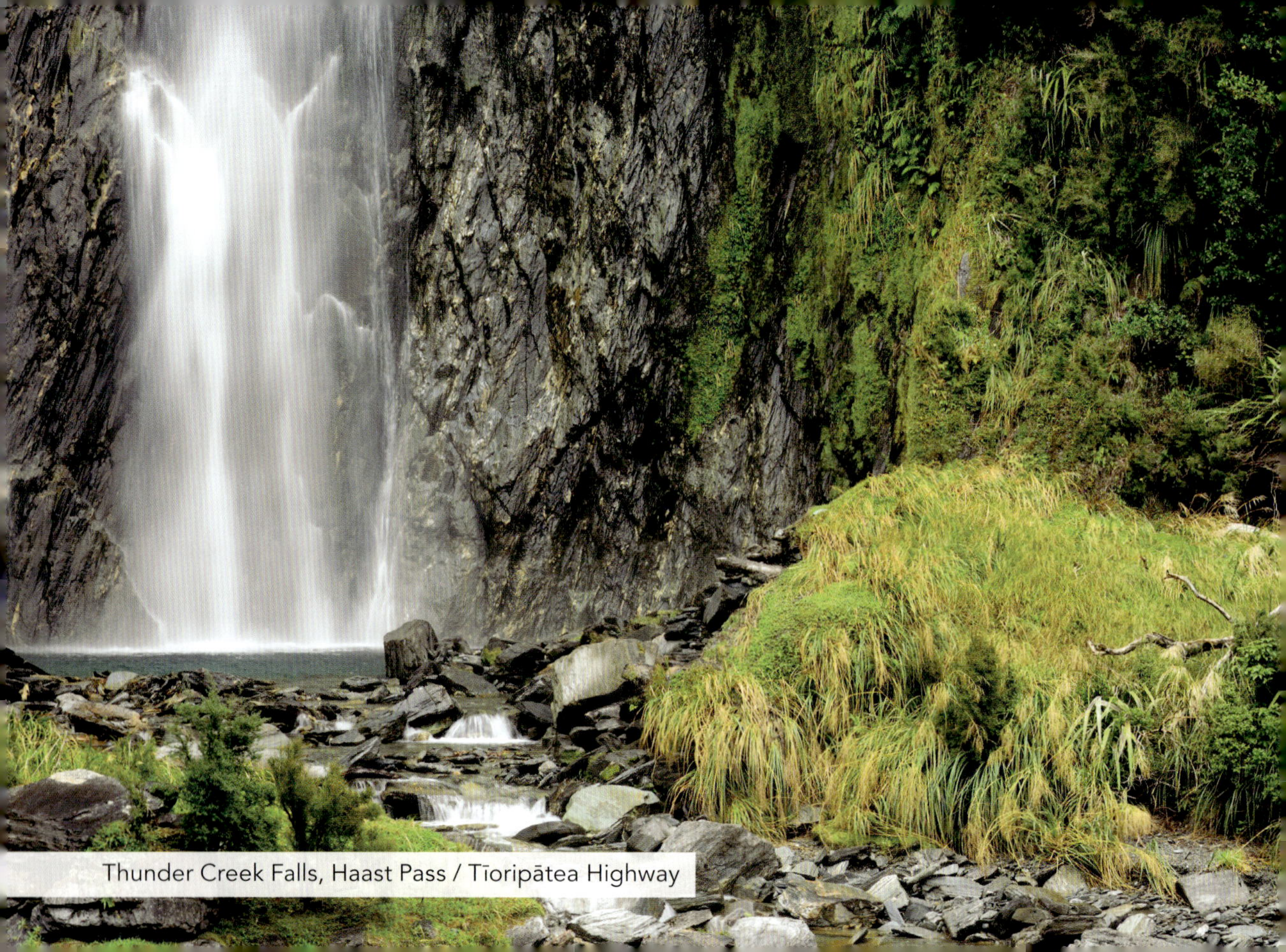

Thunder Creek Falls, Haast Pass / Tīoripātea Highway

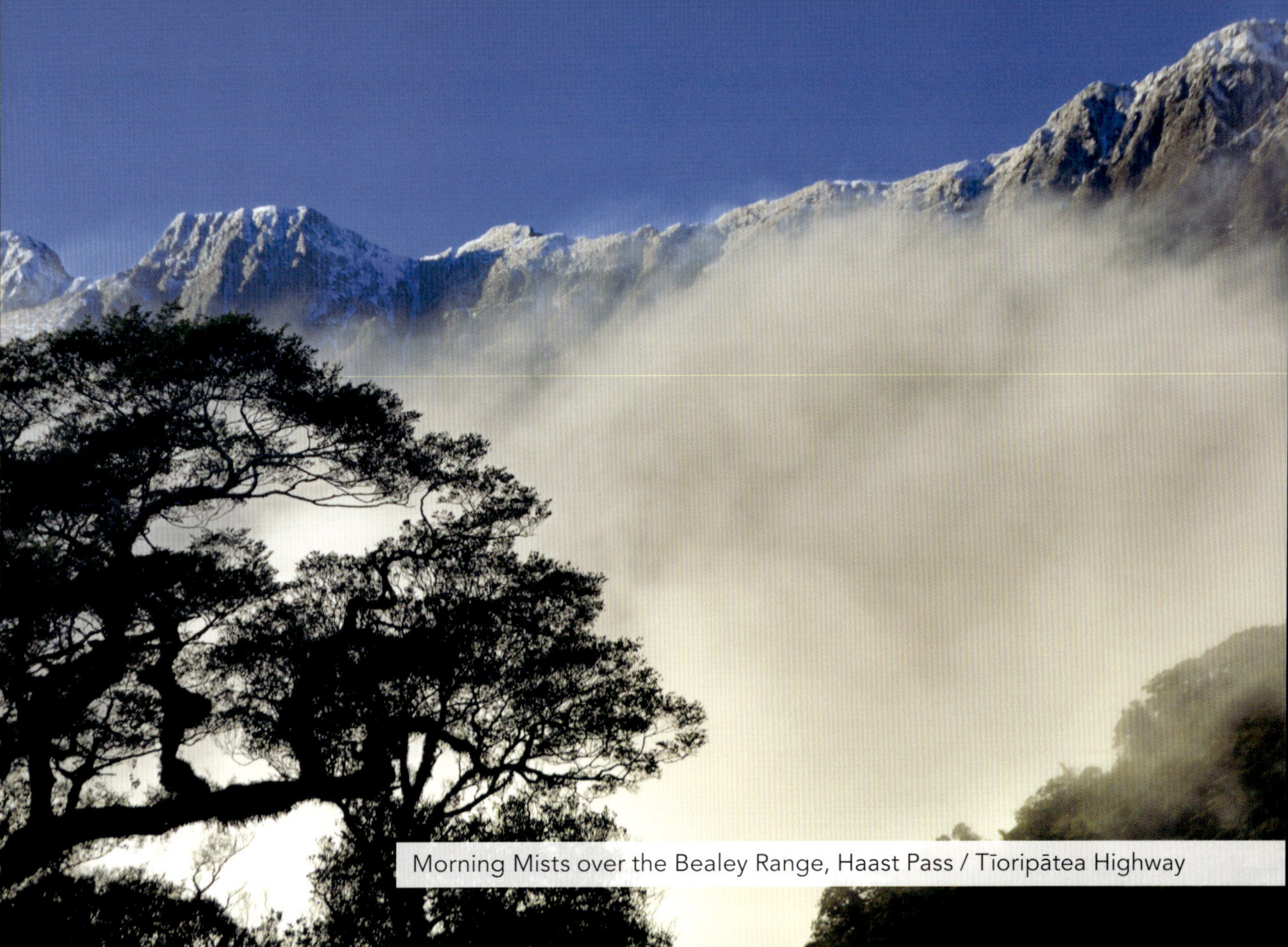

Morning Mists over the Bealey Range, Haast Pass / Tīoripātea Highway

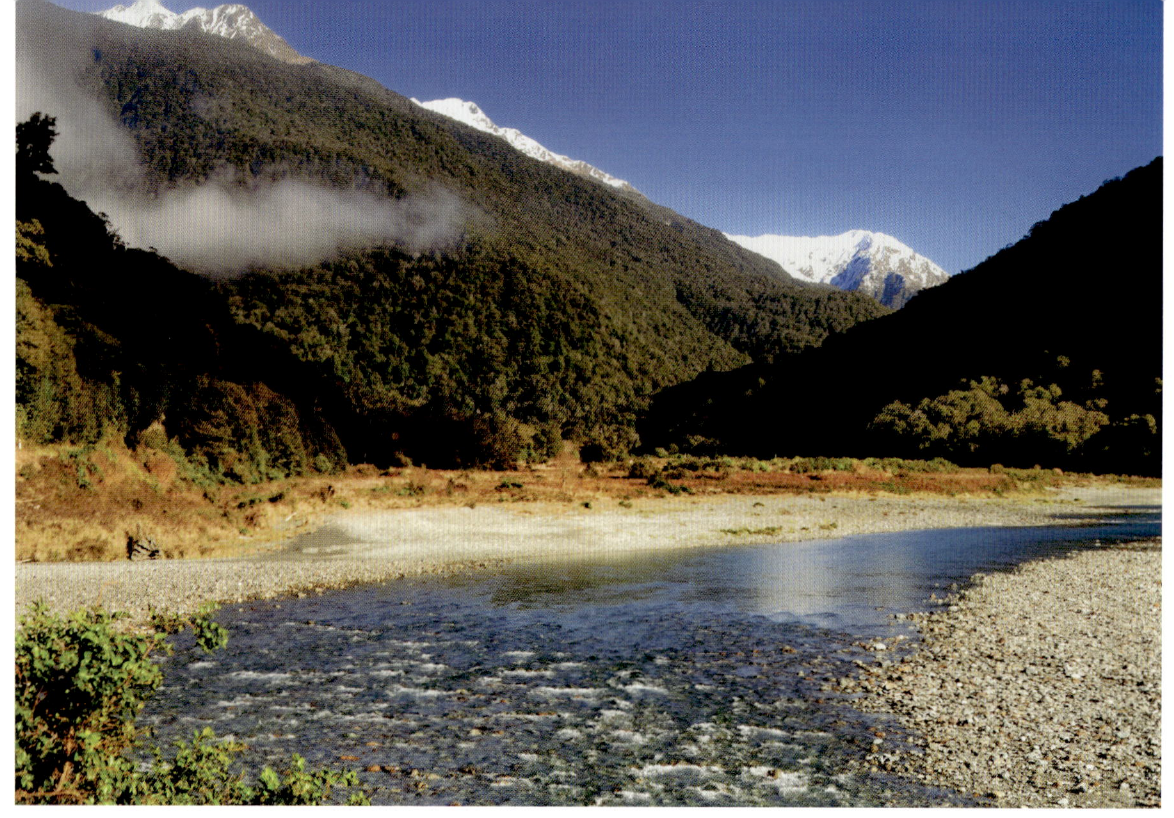

View south from Clarke Bluff of the Haast River / Awarua

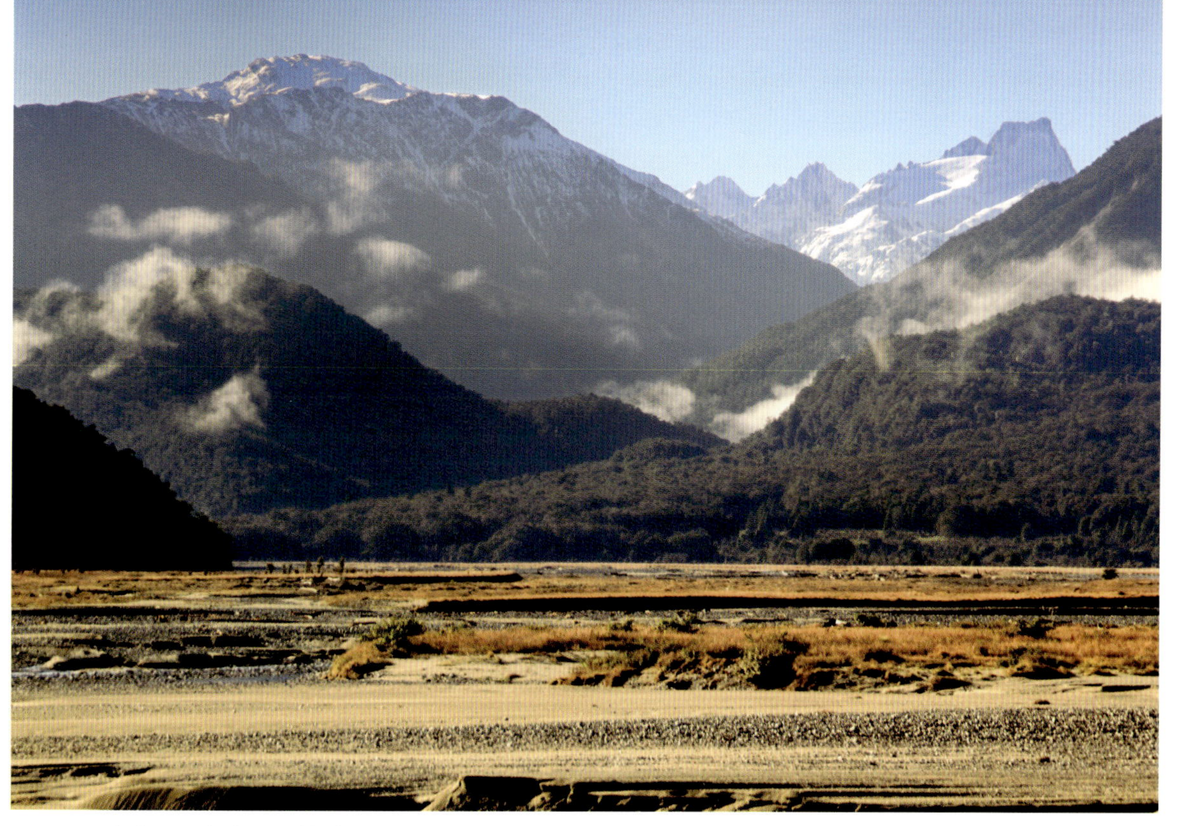

View north from Clarke Bluff of Landsborough Valley at the confluence of the Haast and Landsborough Rivers

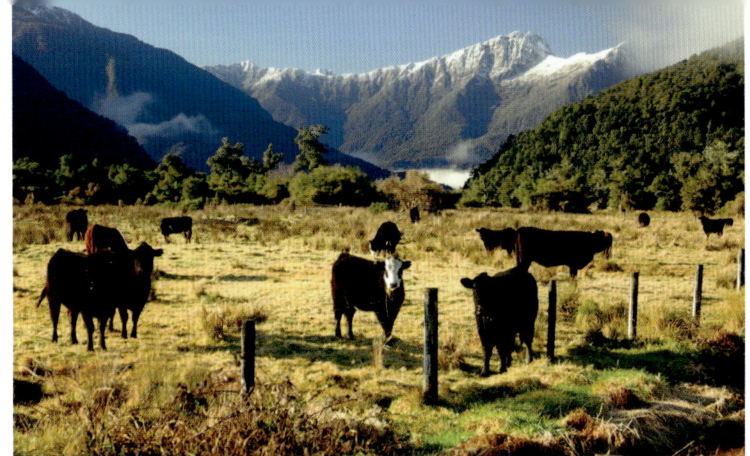

Countryside near Haast (above and below)

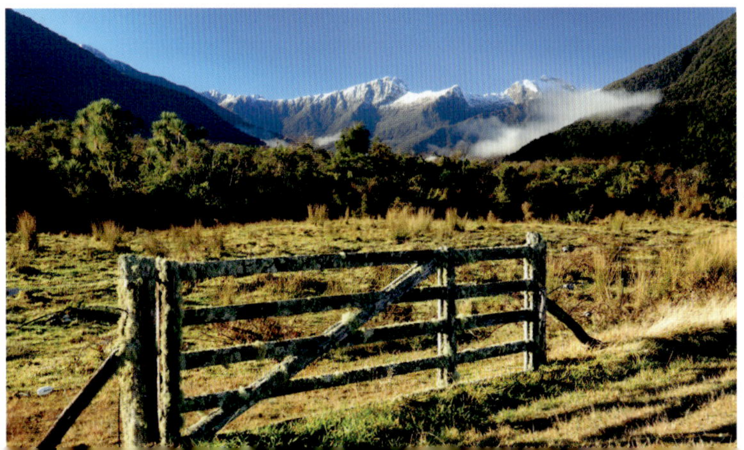

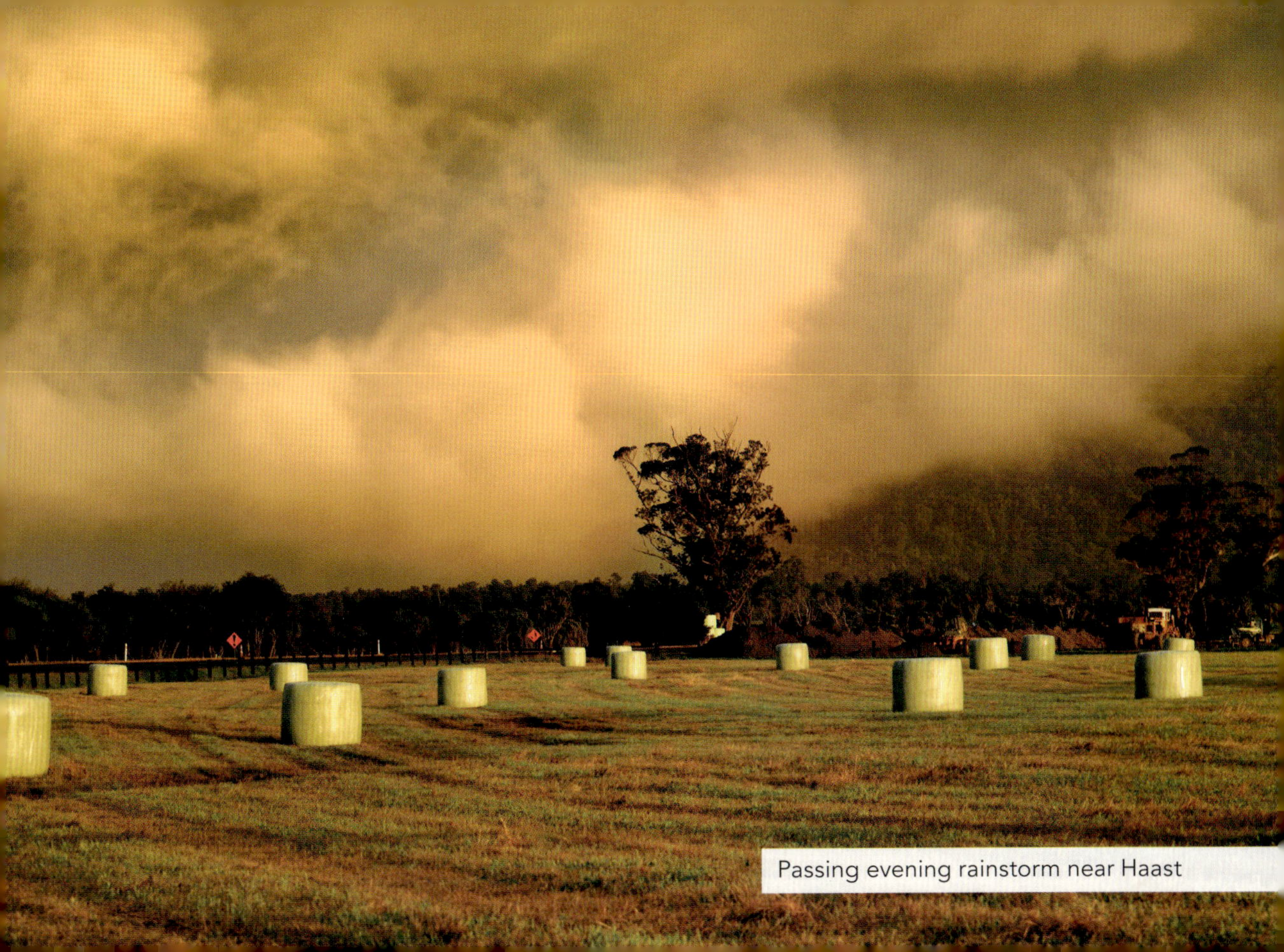

Passing evening rainstorm near Haast

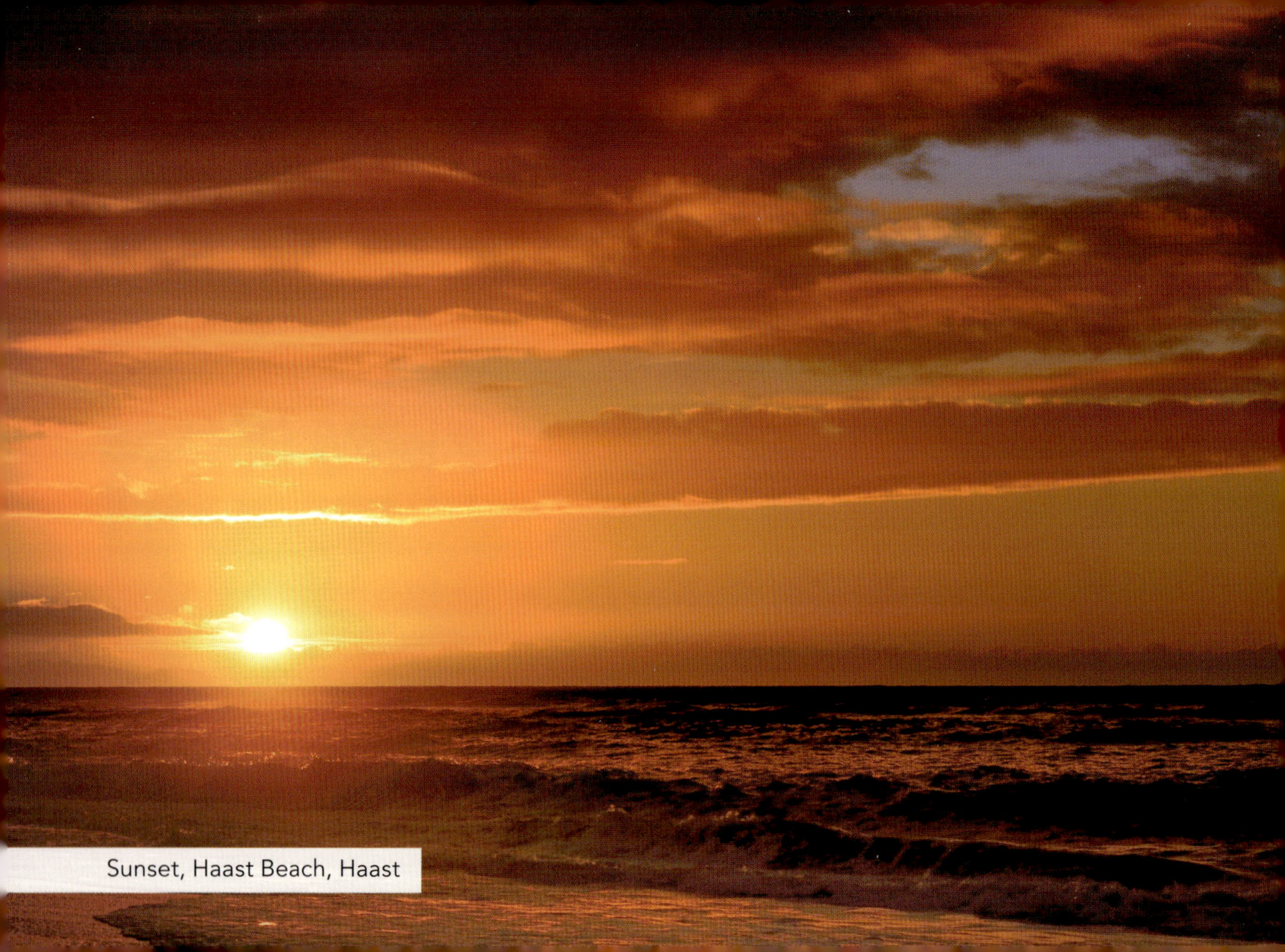

Sunset, Haast Beach, Haast

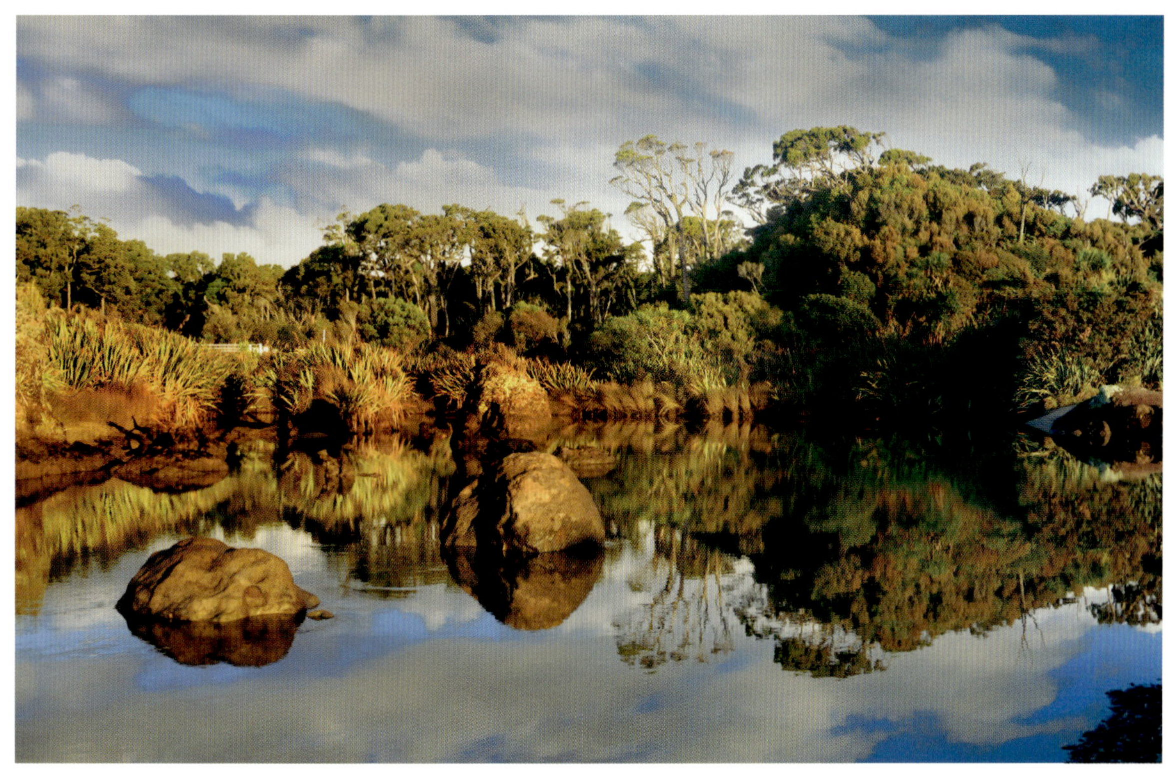

Ship Creek near Haast

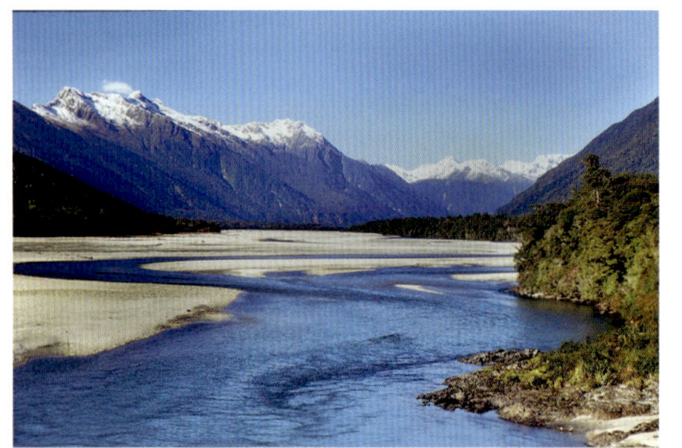

Arawhata River

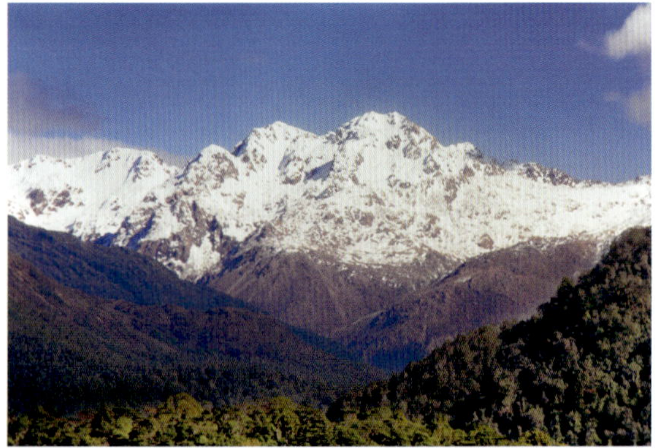

Cascade Valley

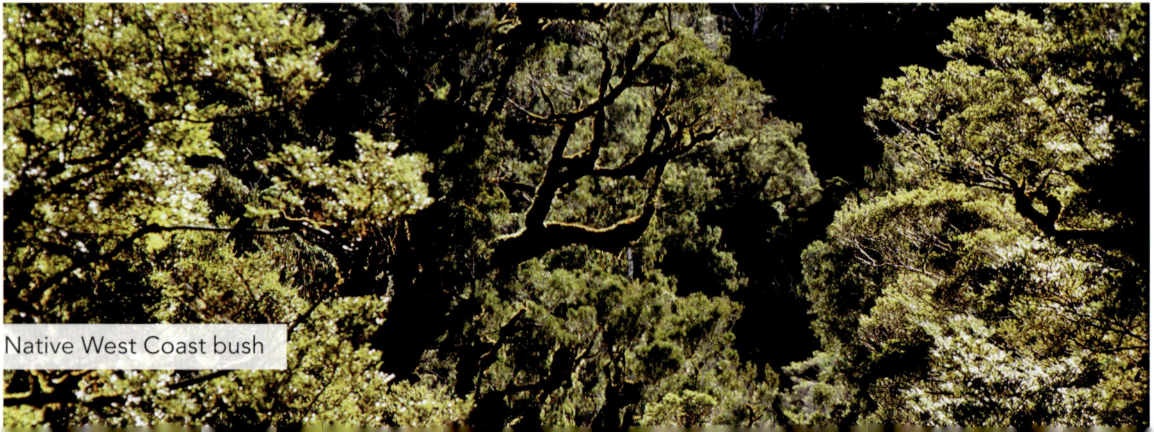

Native West Coast bush

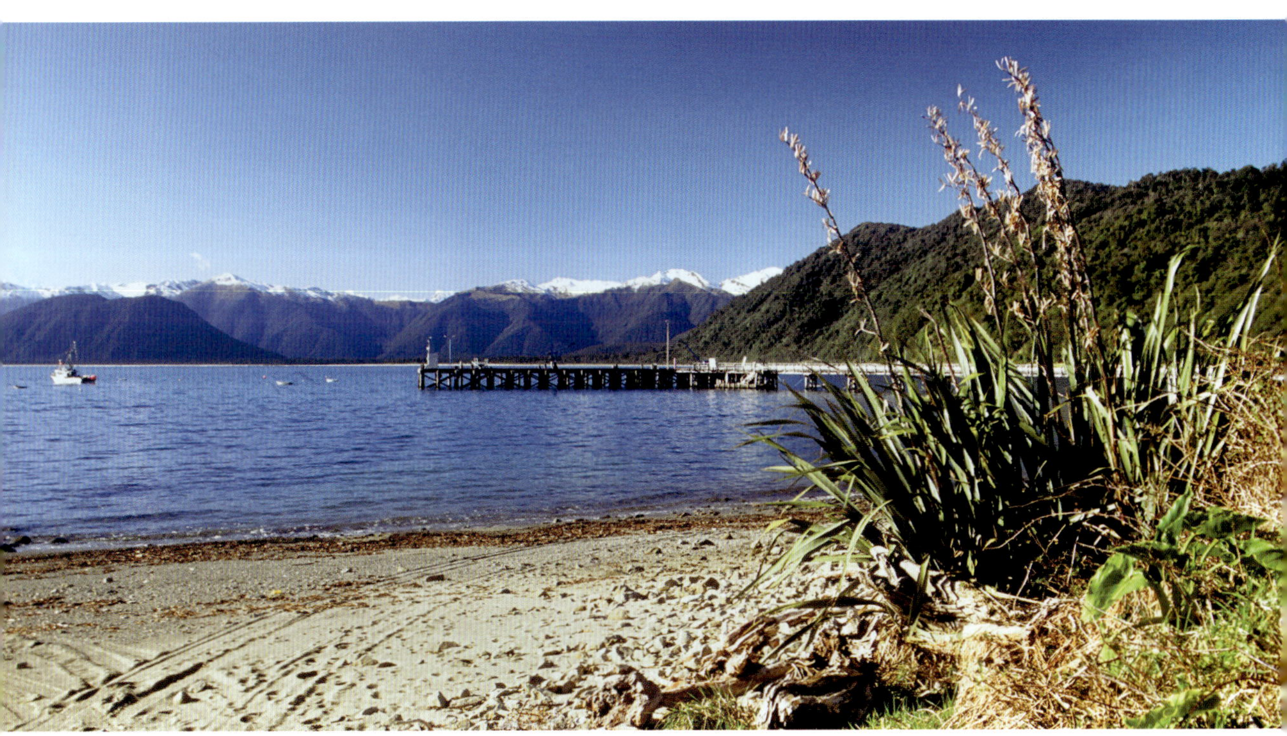

Jackson Bay / Okahu

The Clutha River / Mata-Au and Lake Dunstan

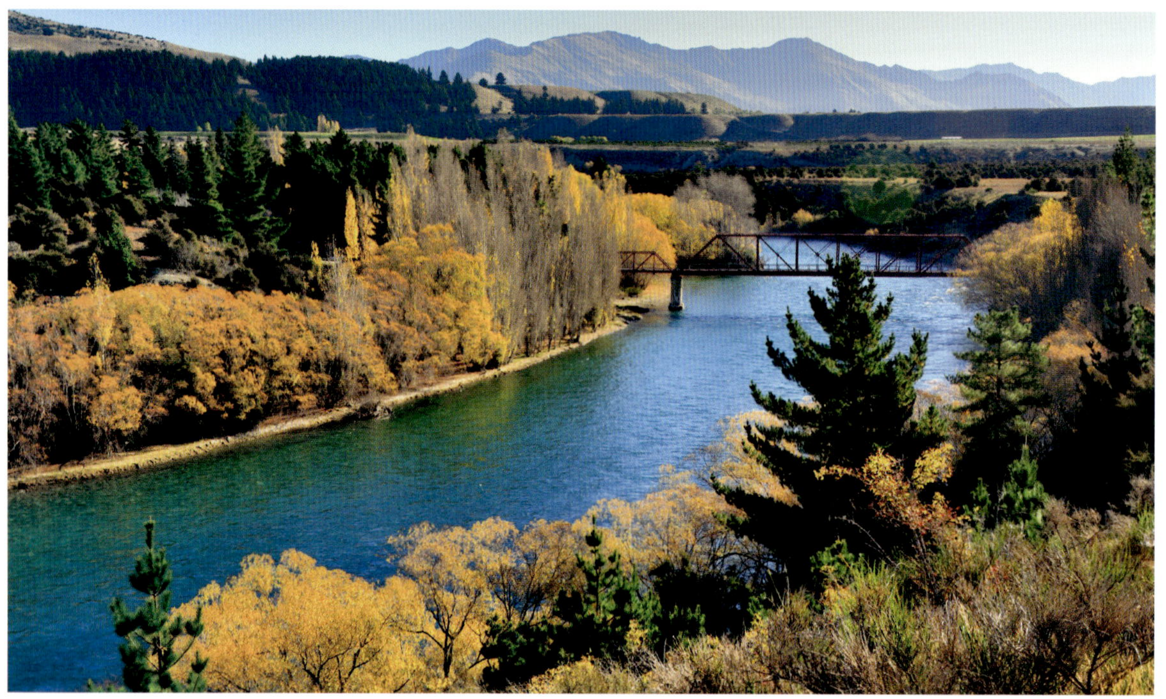

Clutha River / Mata-Au near Luggate

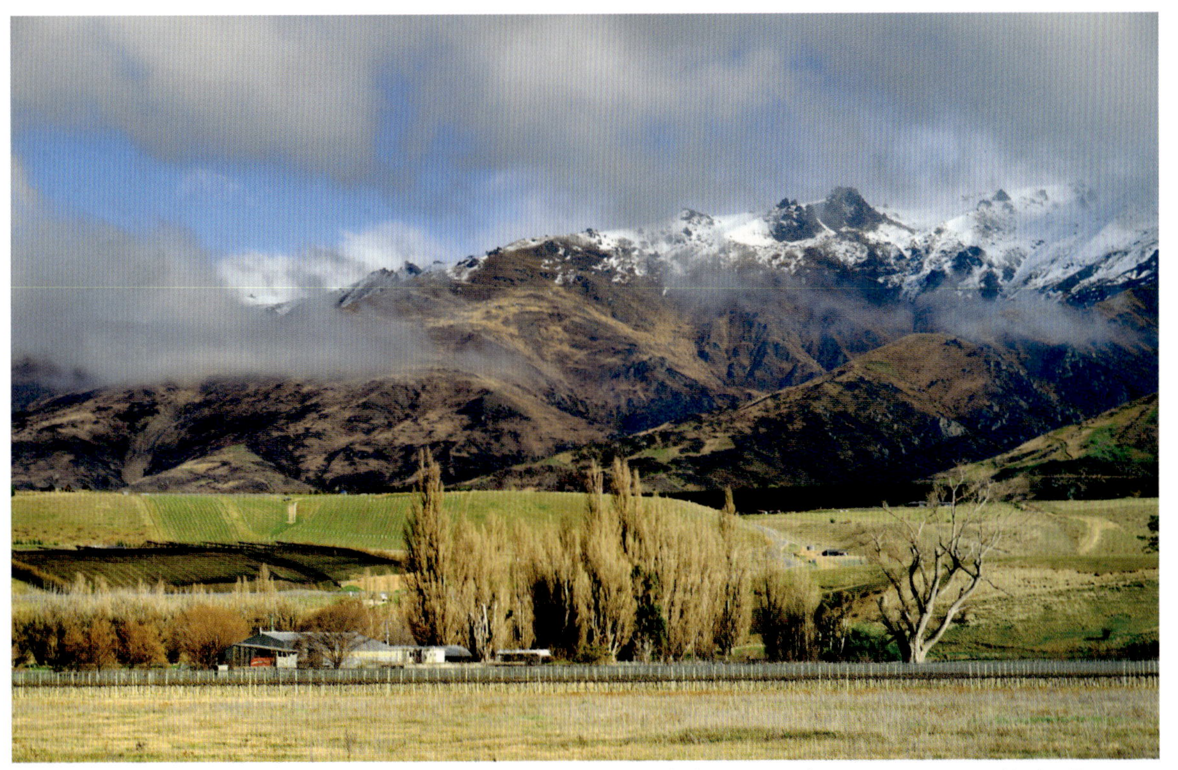

Countryside between the Pisa Range and Lake Dunstan

56

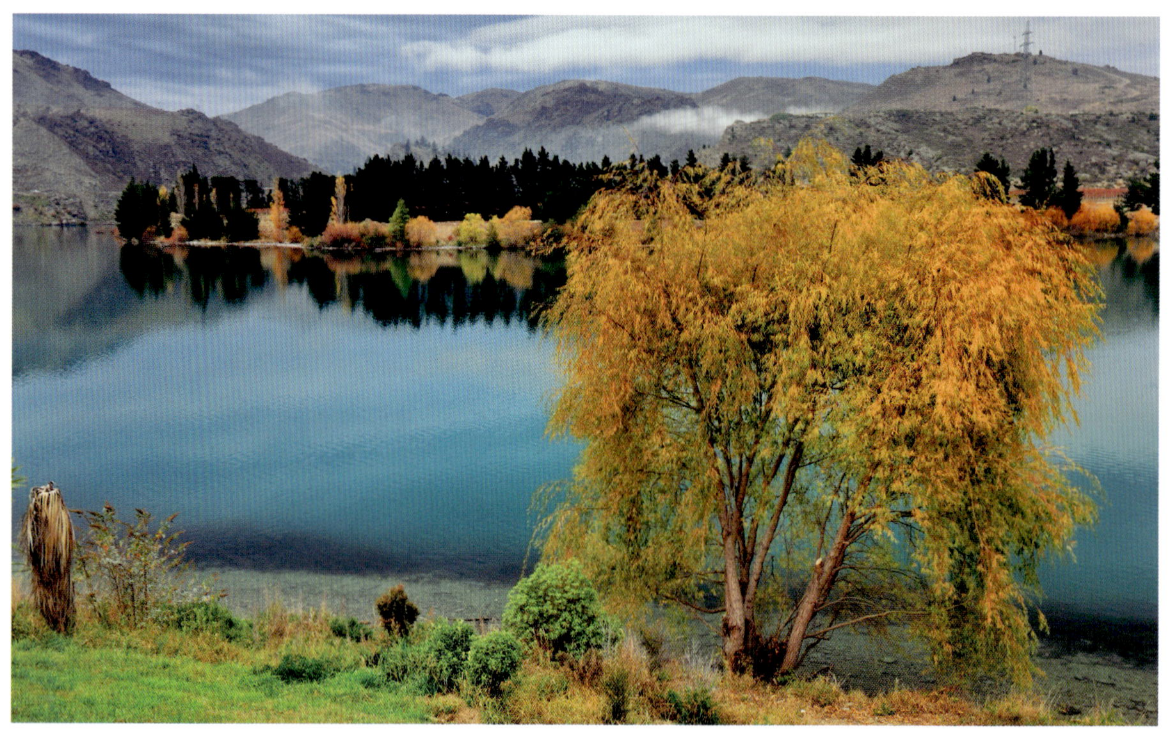

Lakeside, Old Cromwell Town

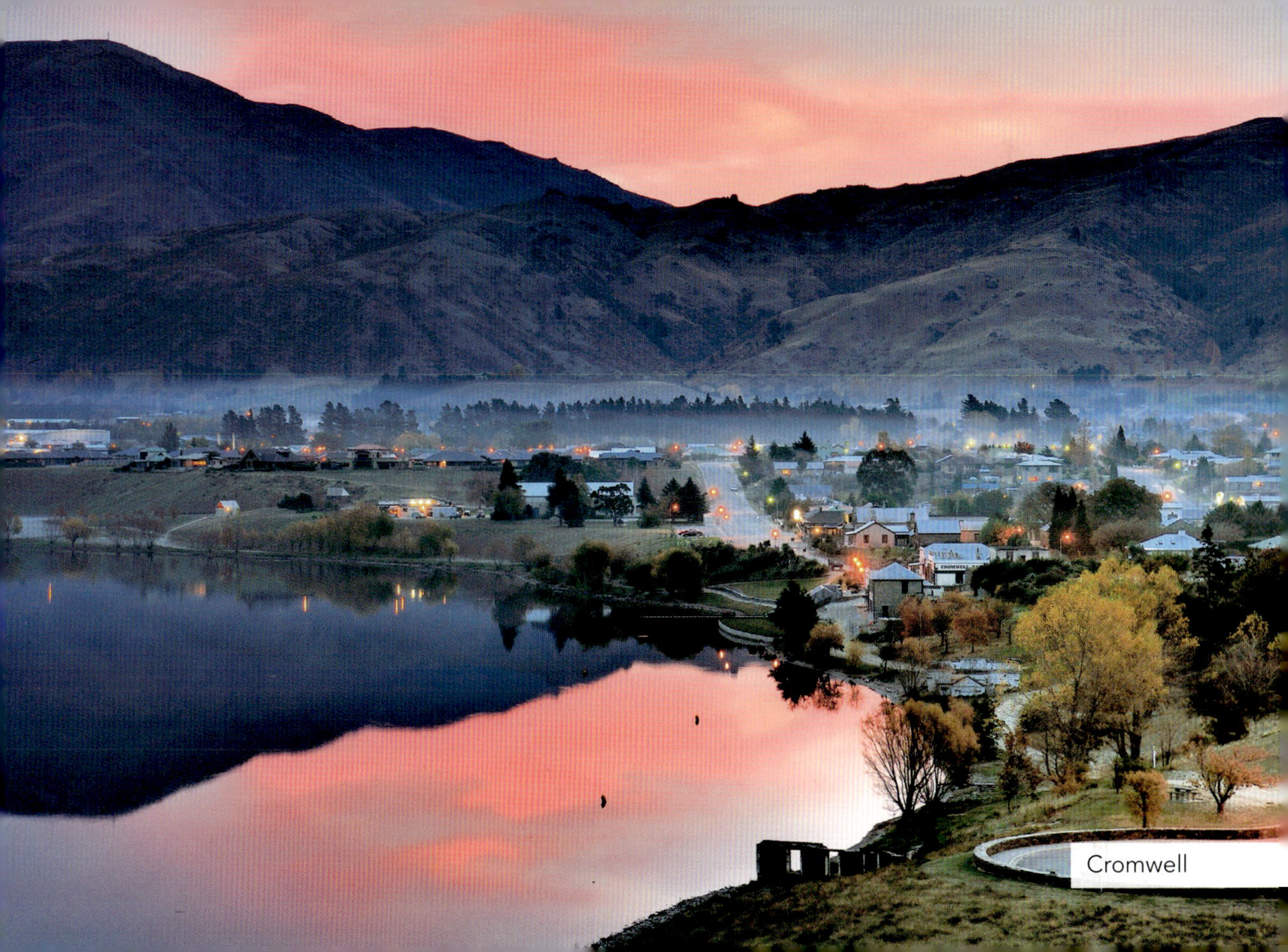
Cromwell

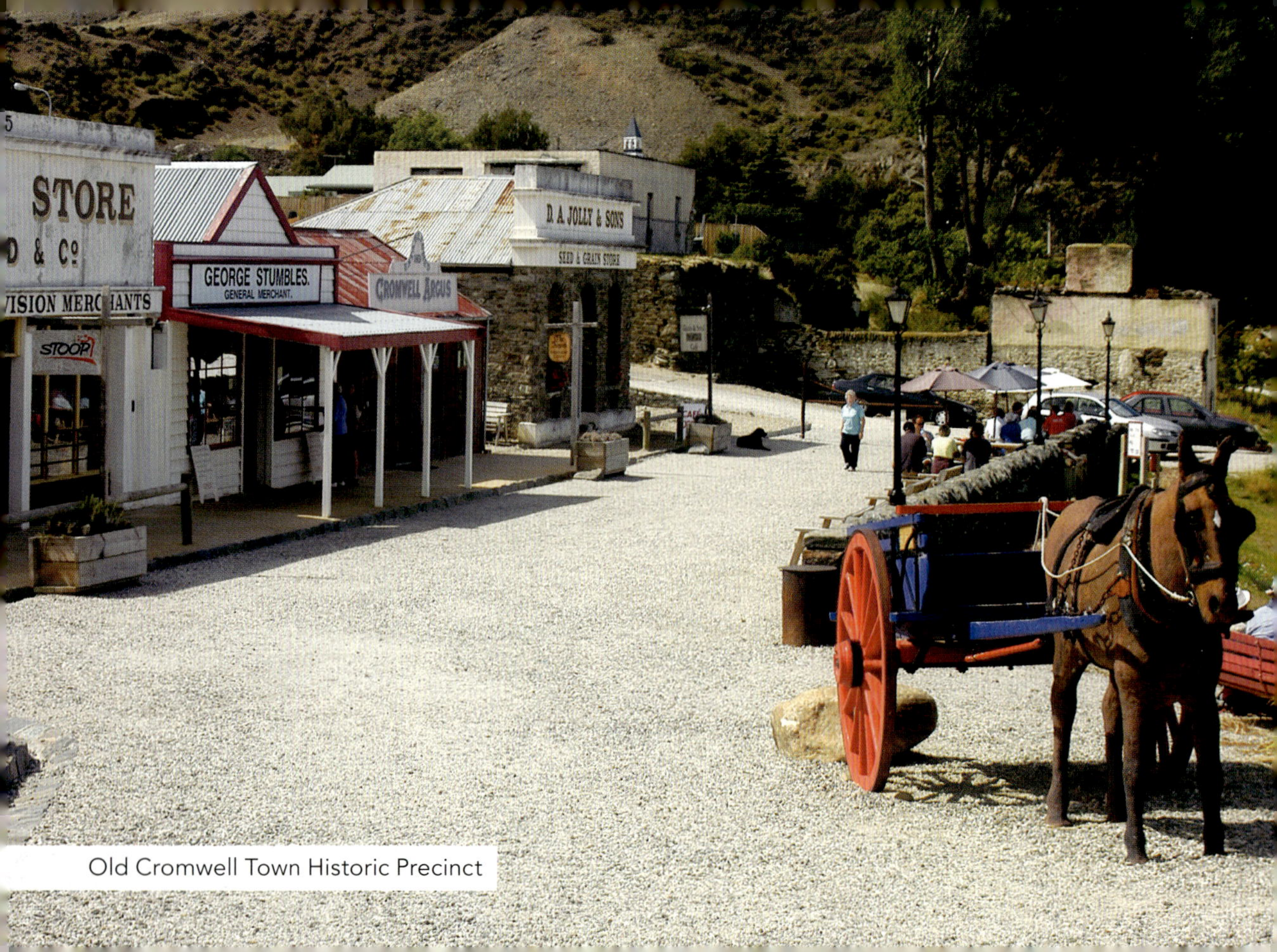

Old Cromwell Town Historic Precinct

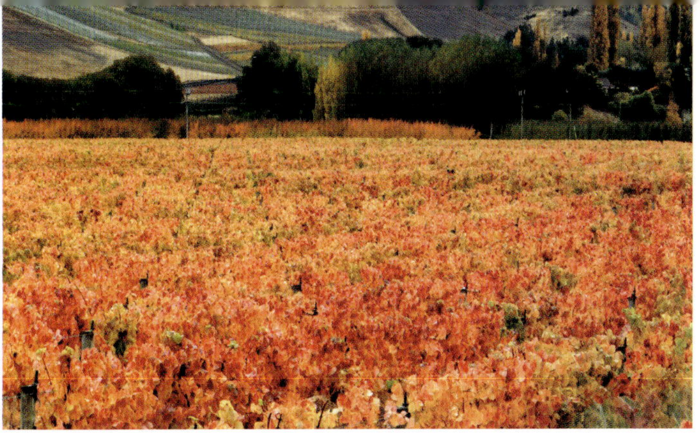

Autumn vineyard, Cromwell

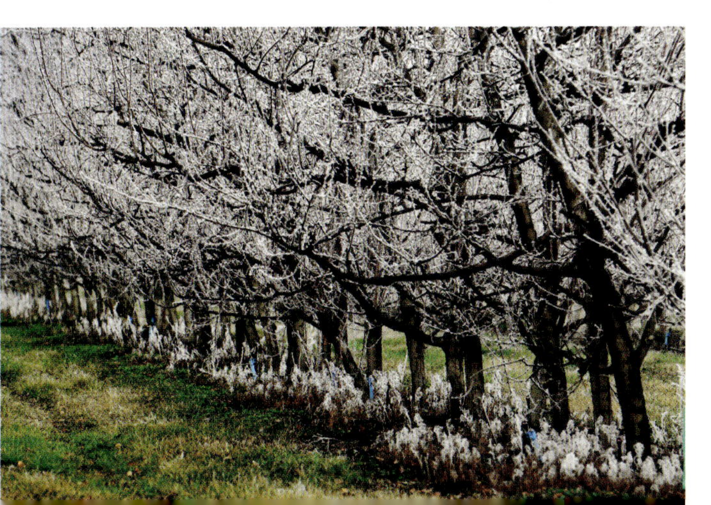

Hoar frost in an apricot orchard, Cromwell

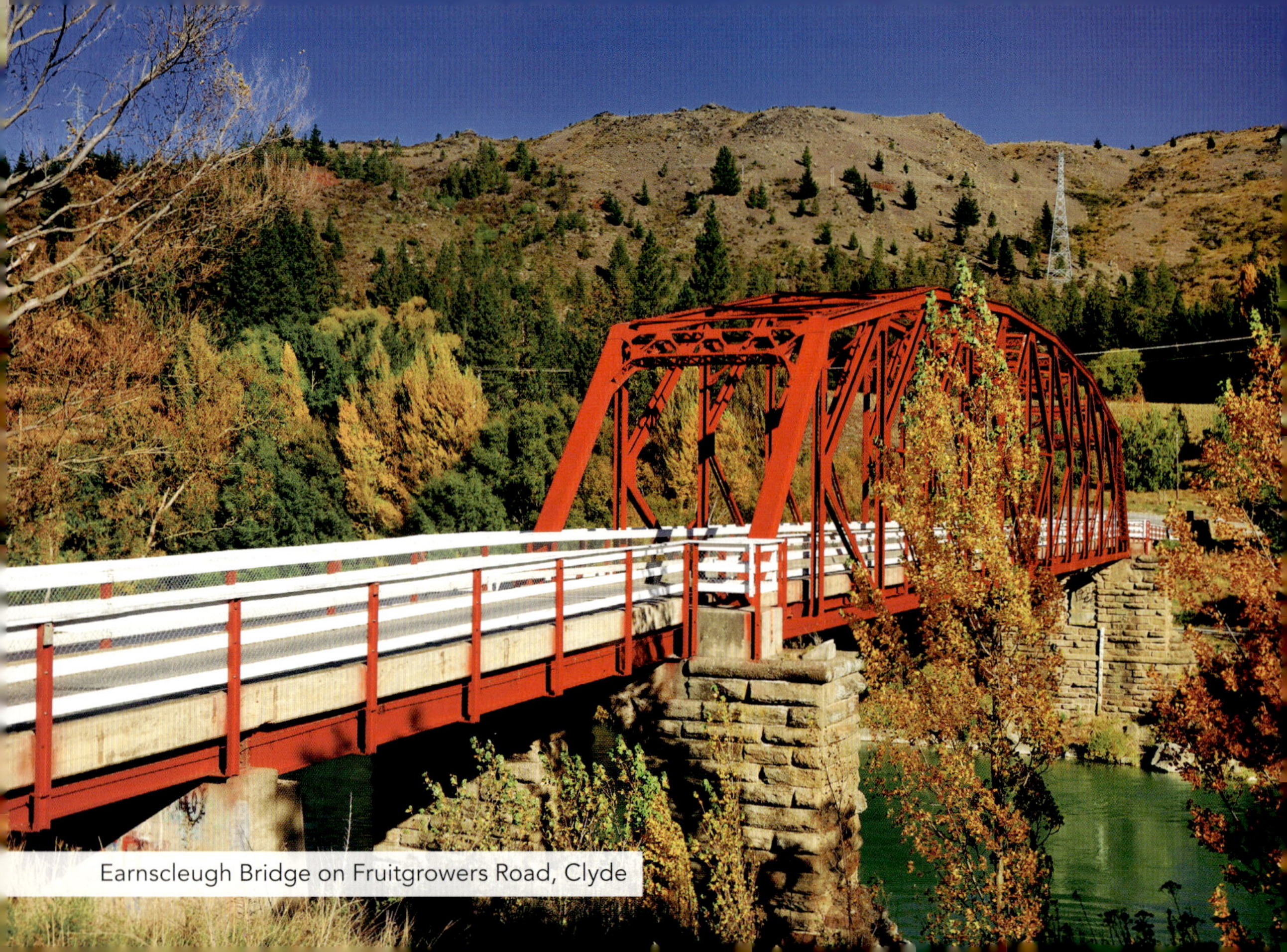

Earnscleugh Bridge on Fruitgrowers Road, Clyde

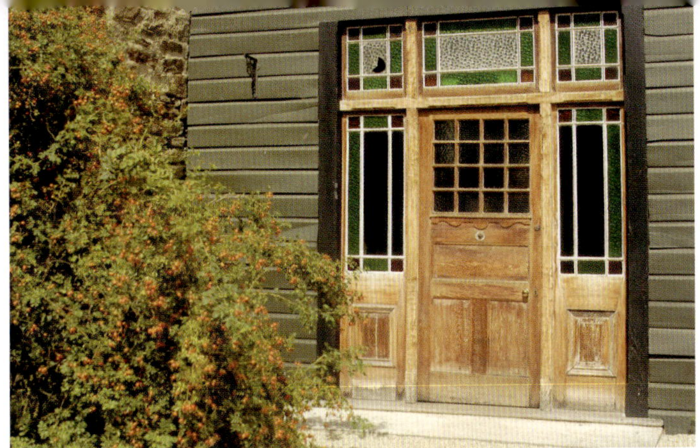

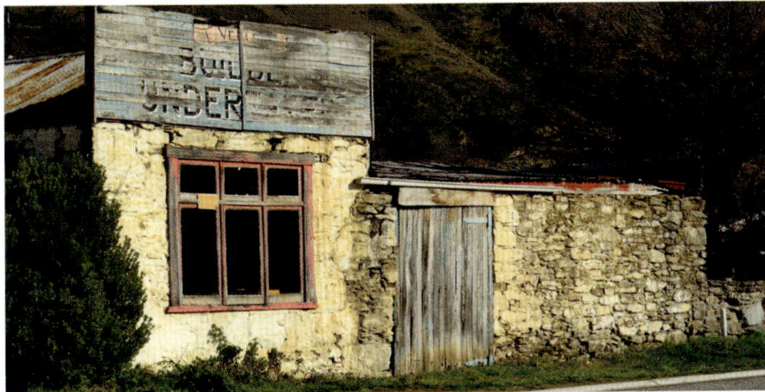

Clyde Central

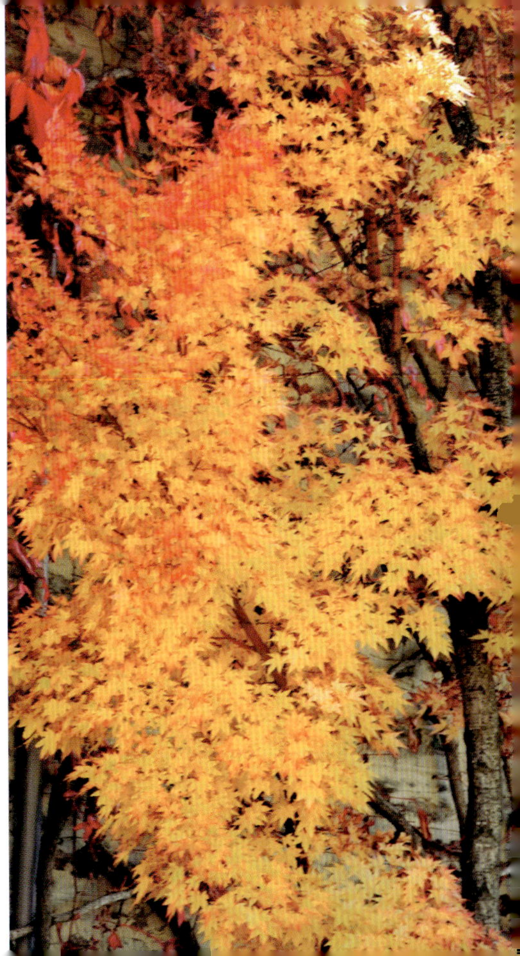

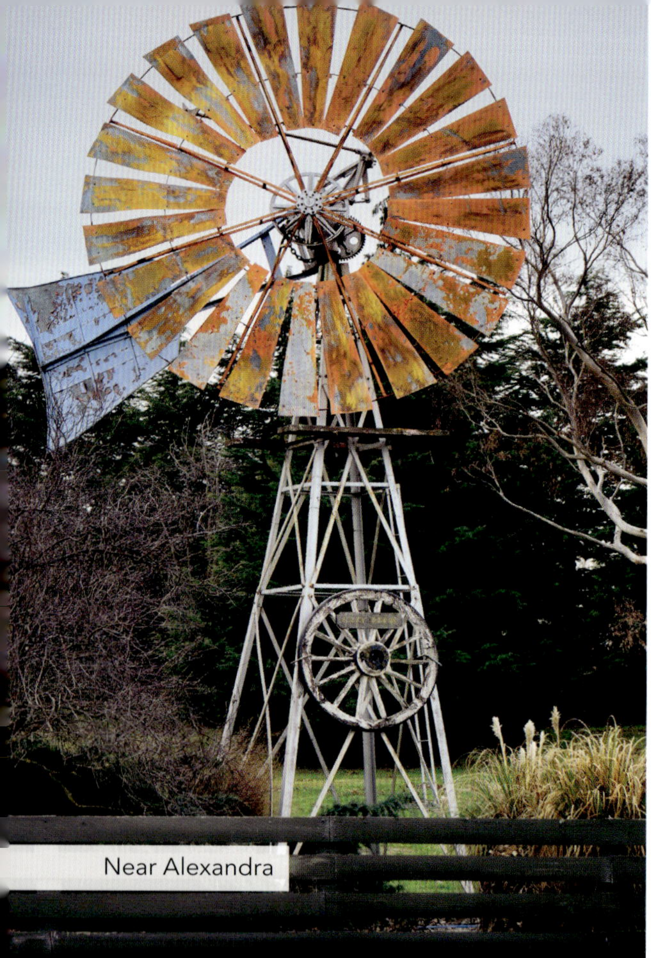

Near Alexandra

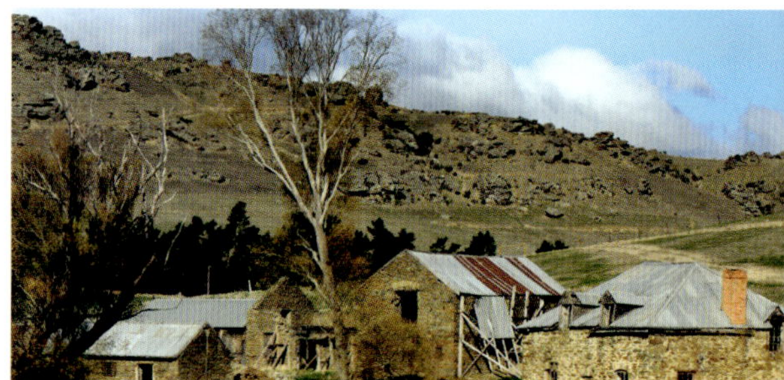

Abandoned farm buildings near Alexandra

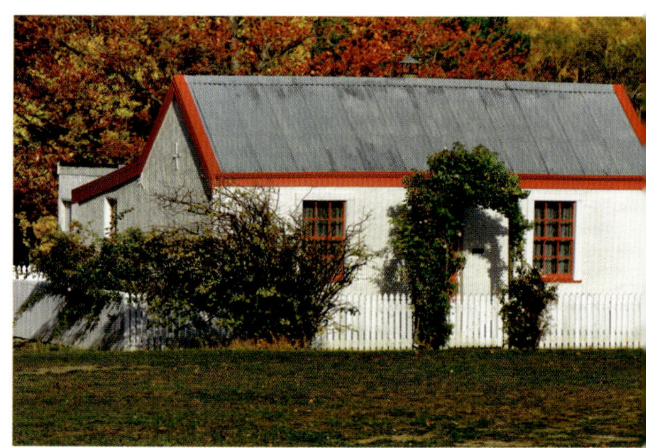

Old cottage near Alexandra

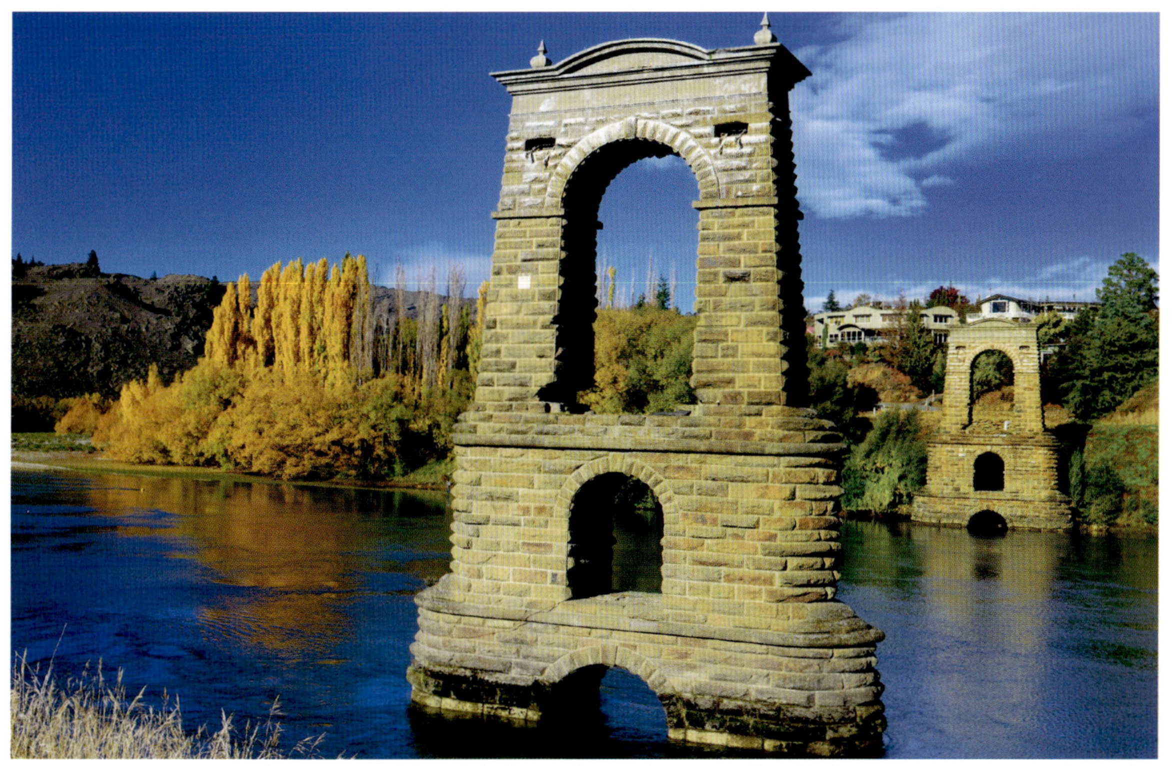

Abutments of the old Alexandra Bridge over the Clutha River / Mata-Au, Alexandra

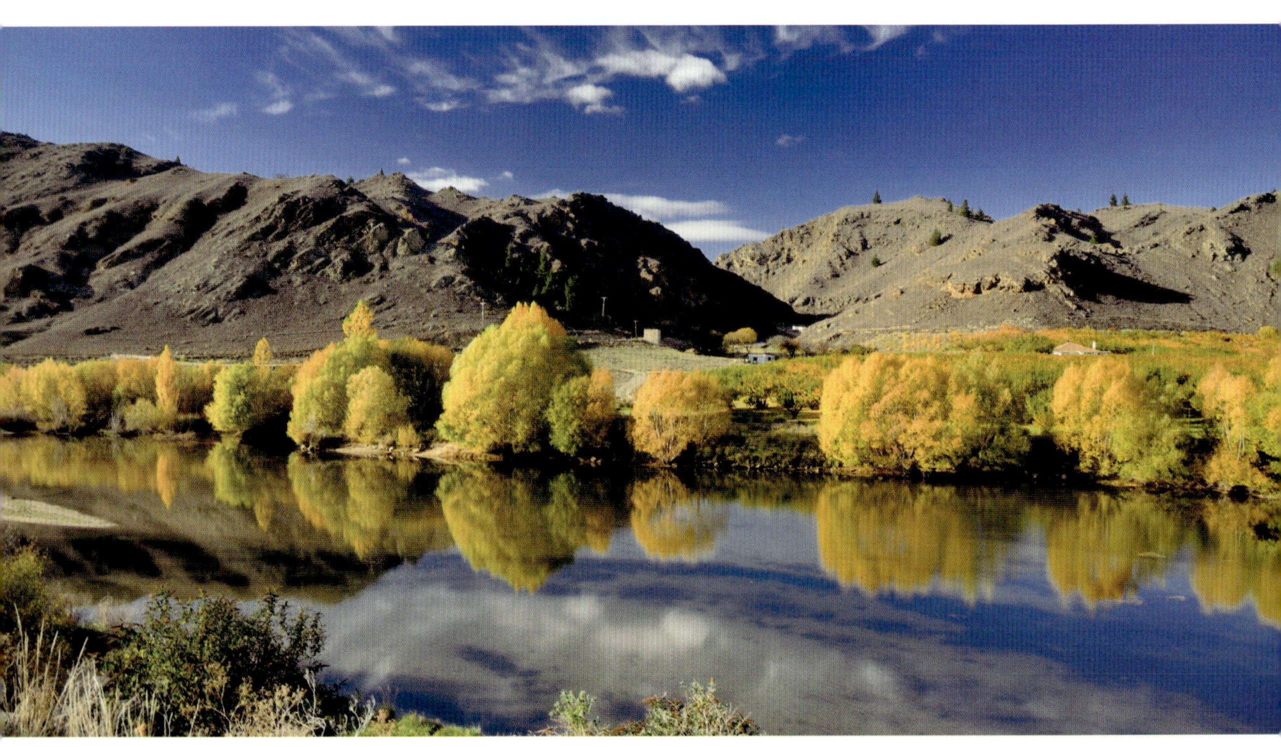

Manuherikia River, Alexandra

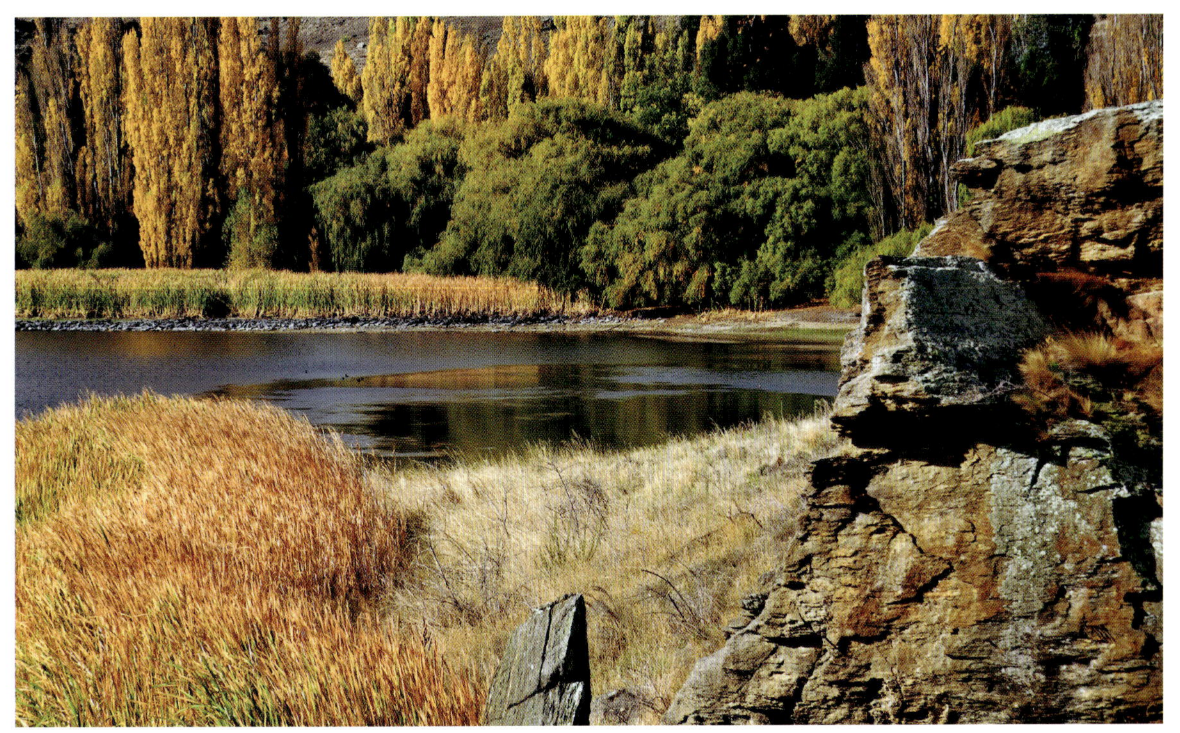

Butchers Dam near Alexandra

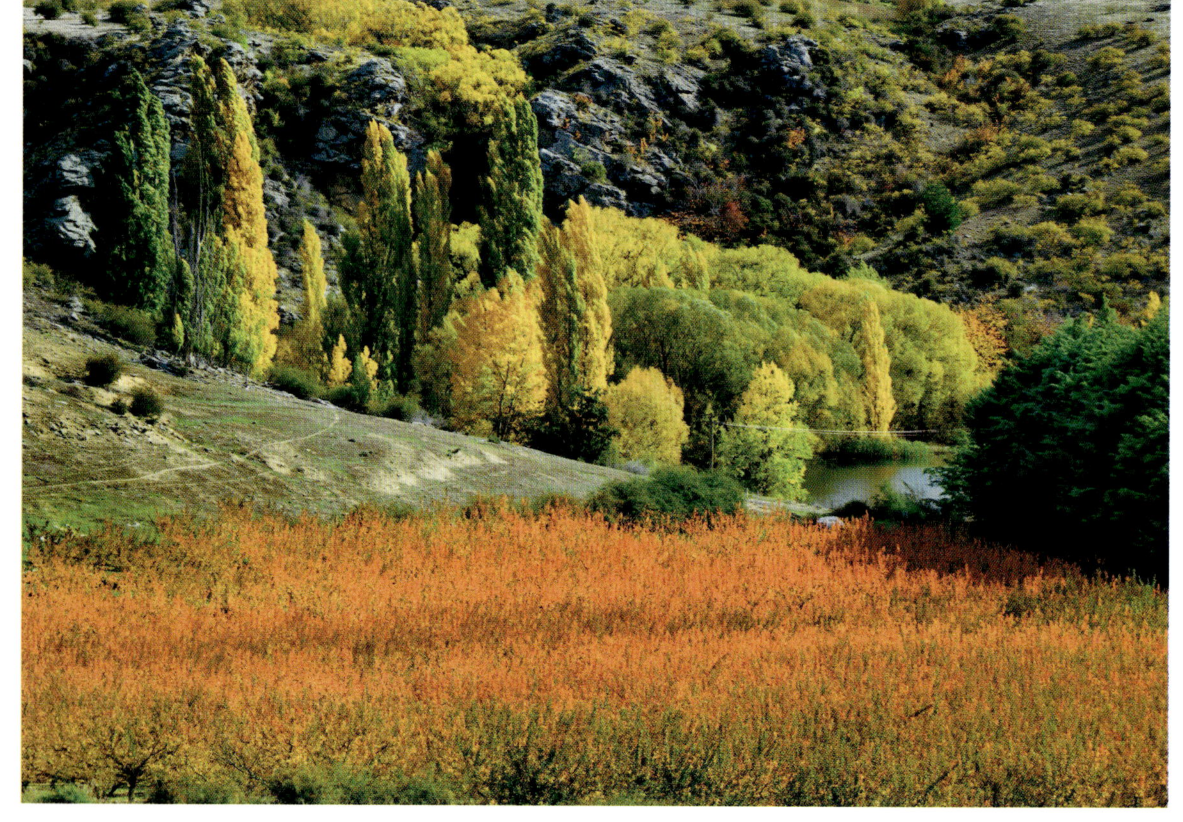

Countryside near Conroys Dam, Earnscleugh

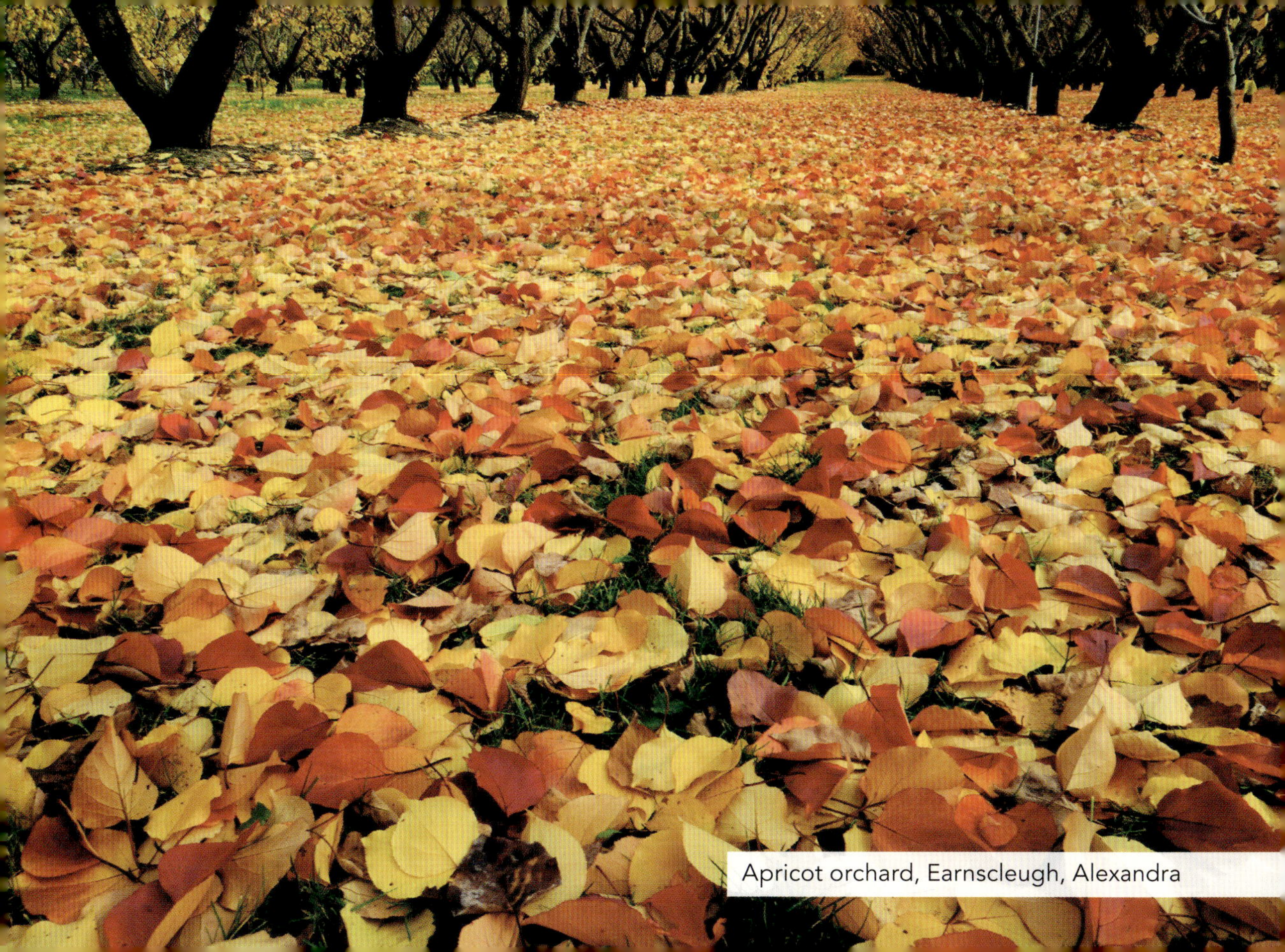

Apricot orchard, Earnscleugh, Alexandra

Bannockburn

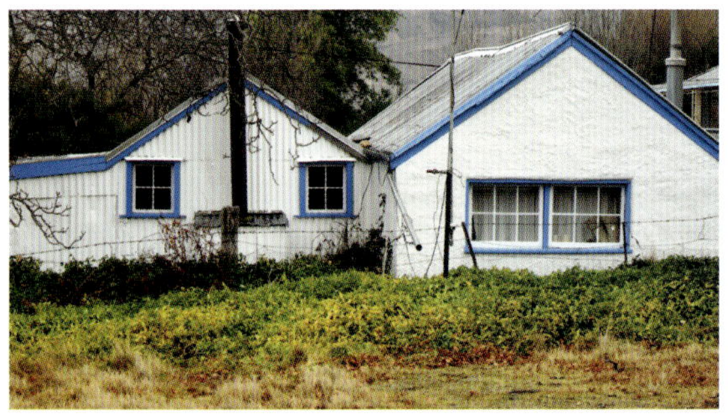

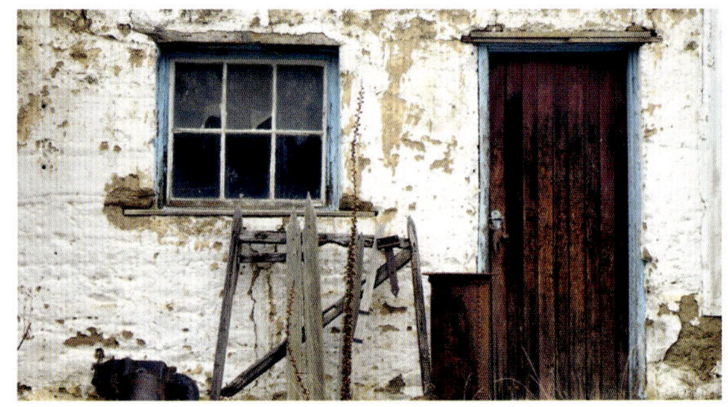

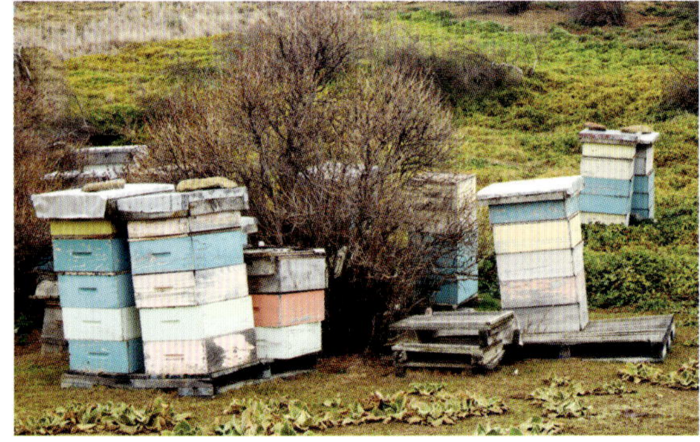

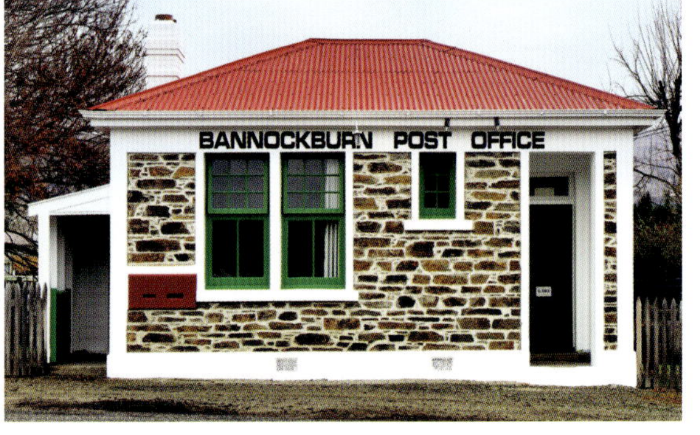

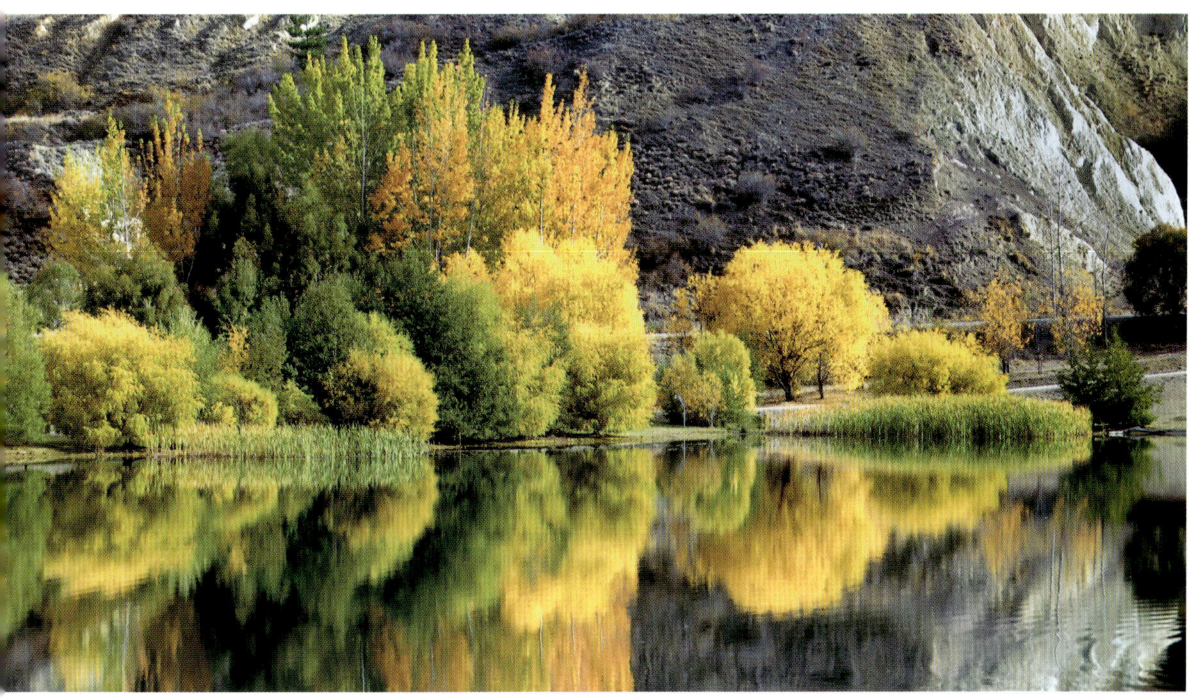

Autumn reflections in the Kawarau River, Bannockburn

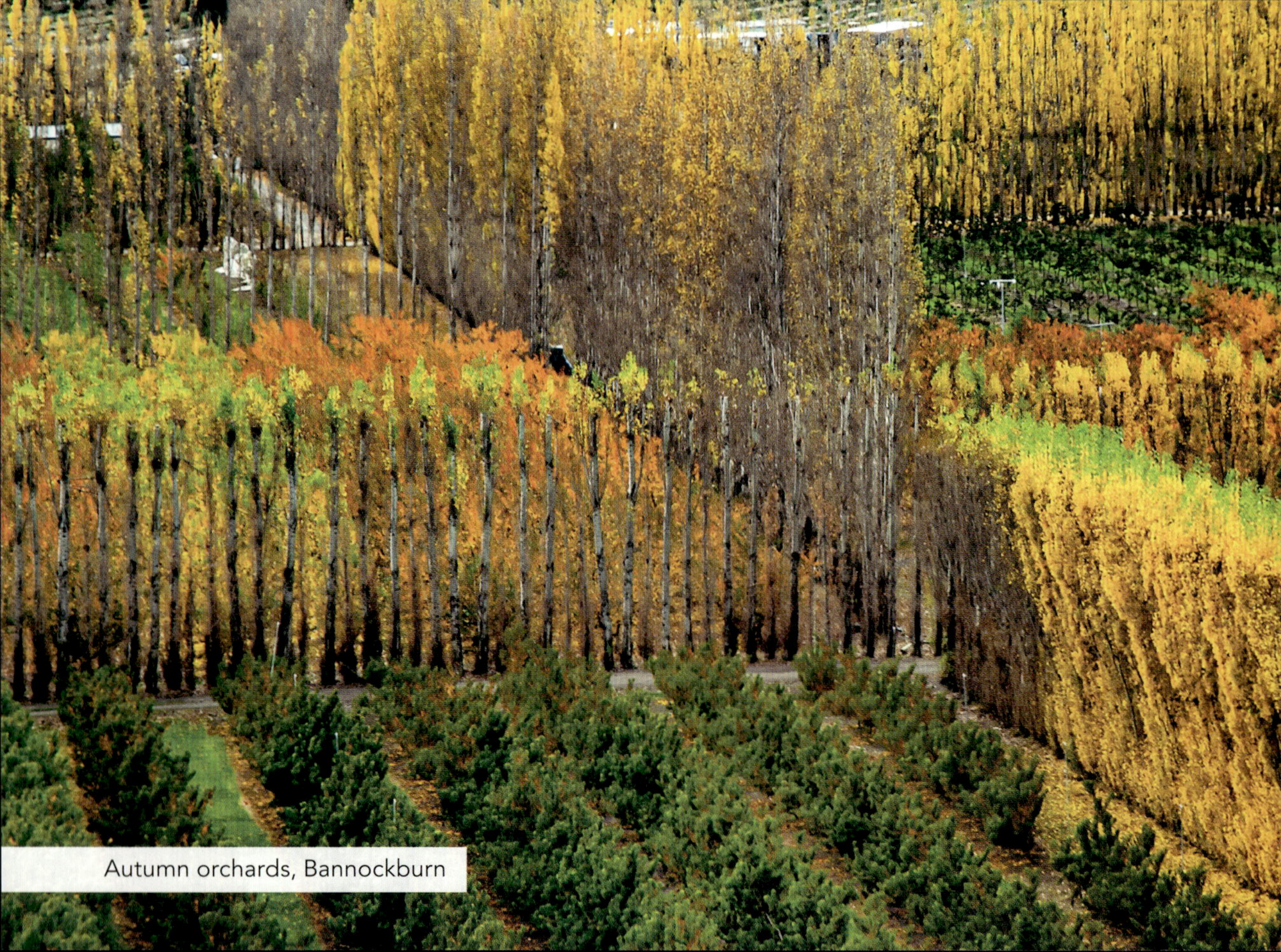

Autumn orchards, Bannockburn

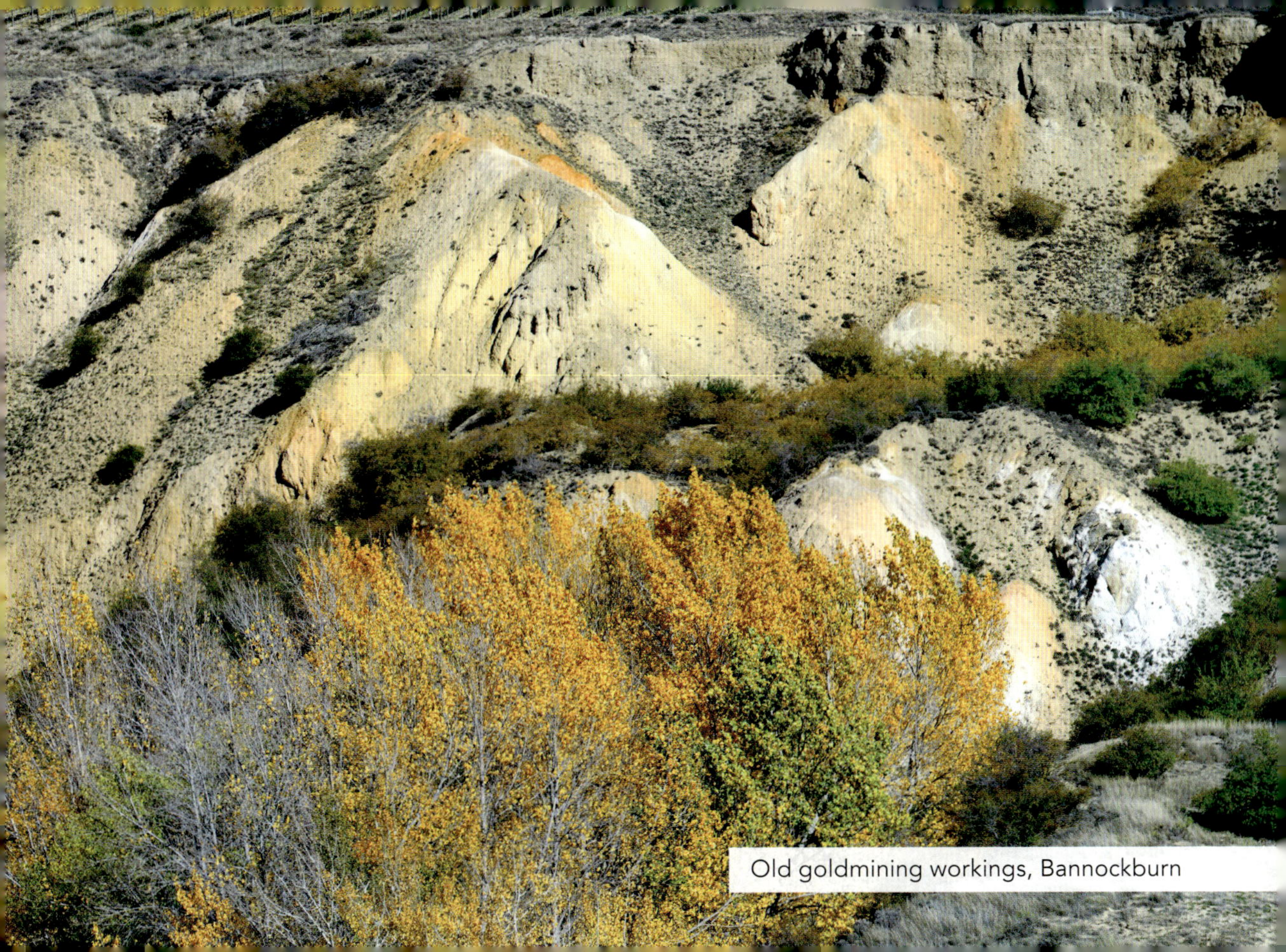

Old goldmining workings, Bannockburn

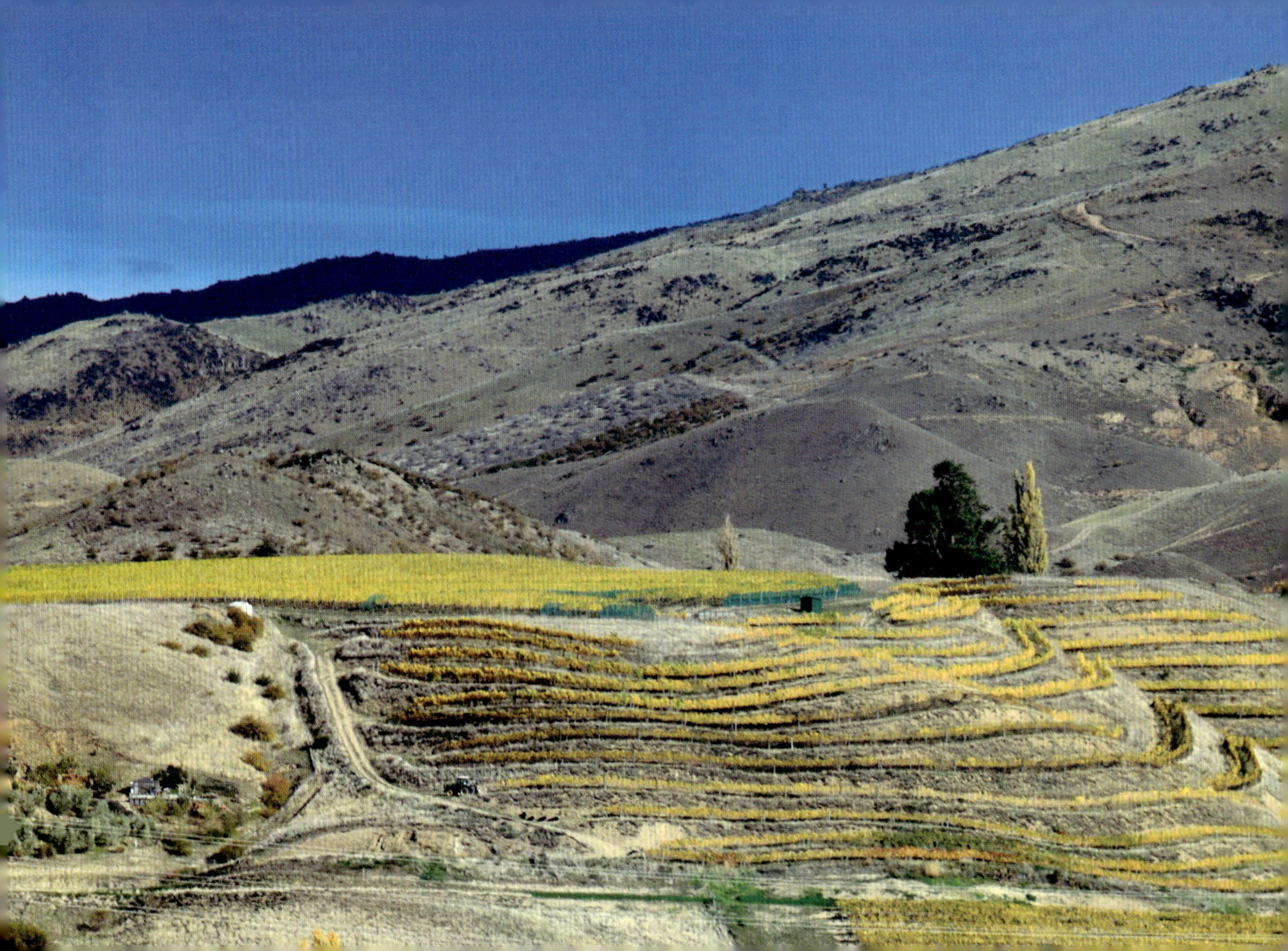

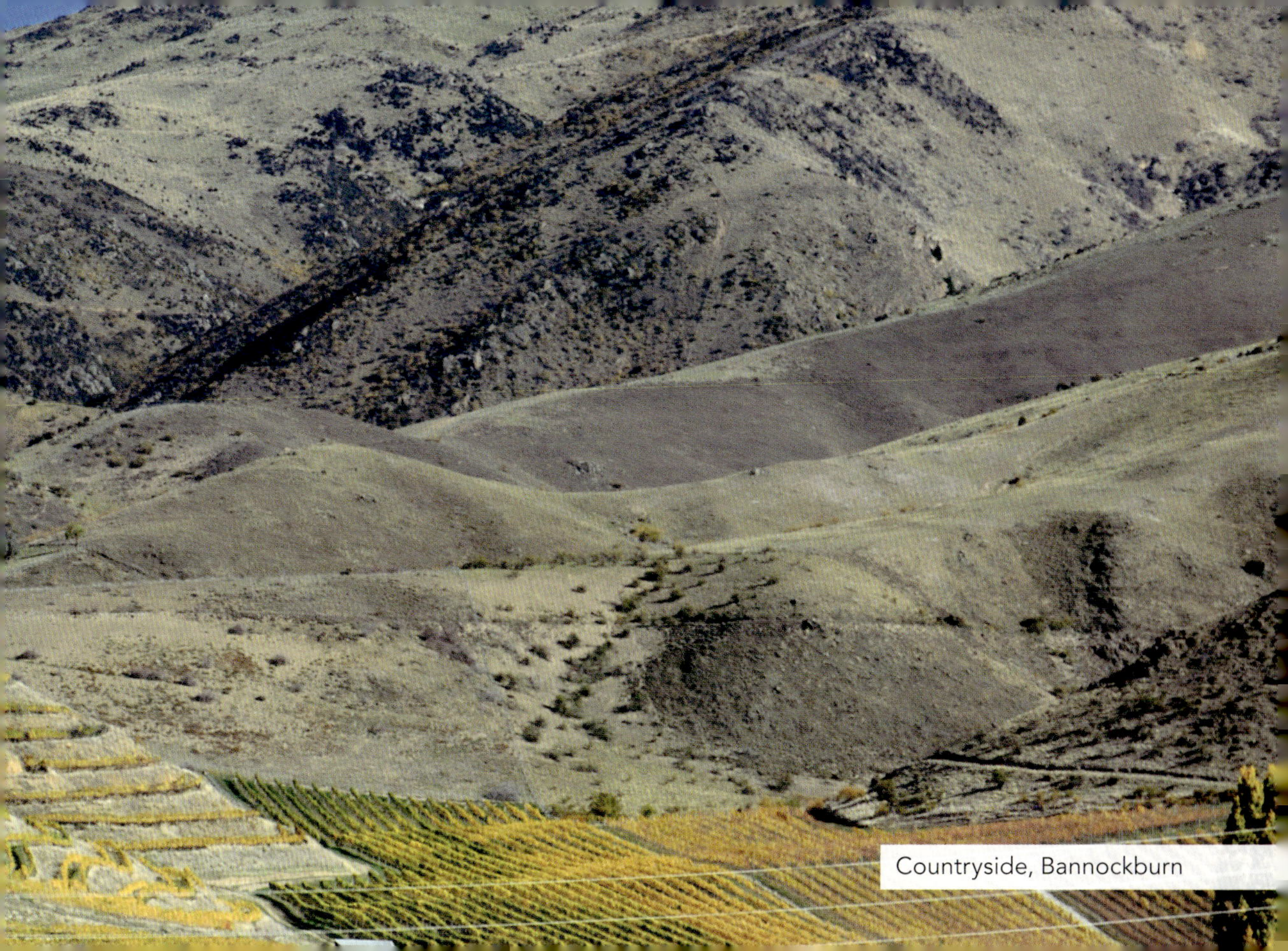

Countryside, Bannockburn

Kiwi As . . . around Queenstown

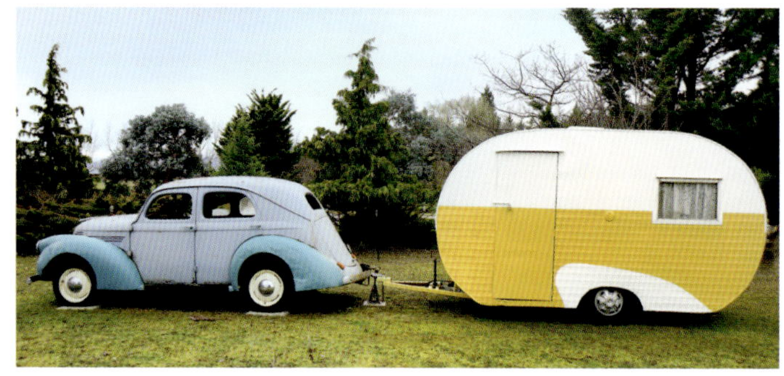

Old car and vintage caravan near Alexandra

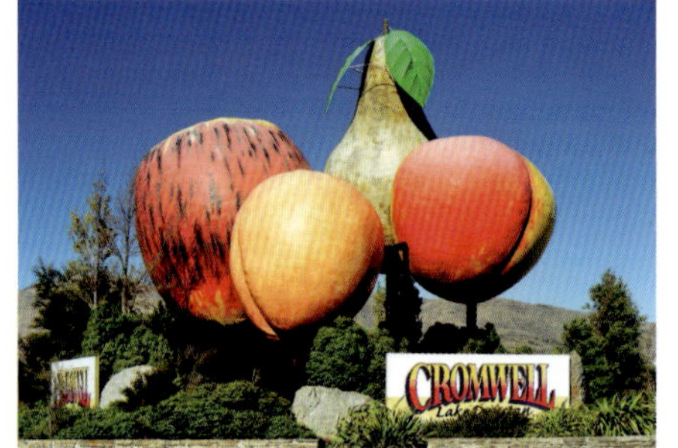

Fruit sign, Cromwell

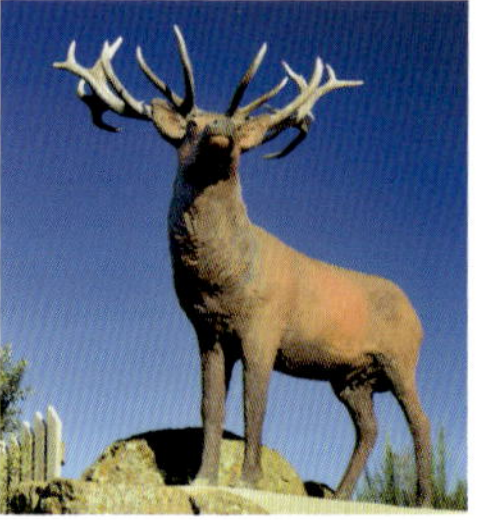

Stag statue, Mossburn

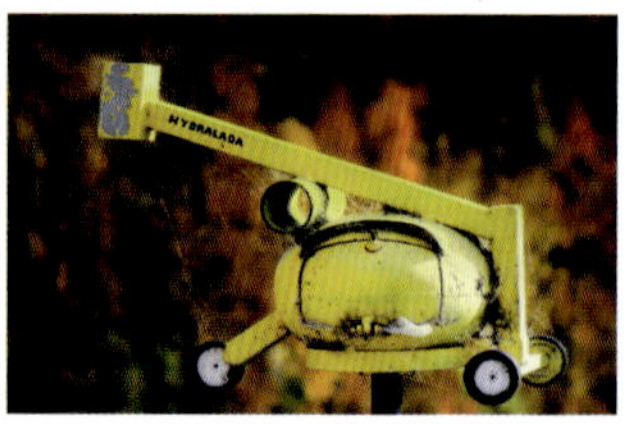

Rural mailbox, Earnscleugh

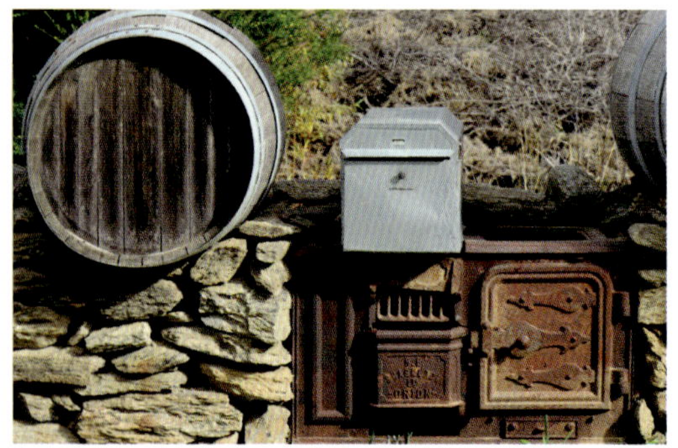

Postal centre near Earnscleugh

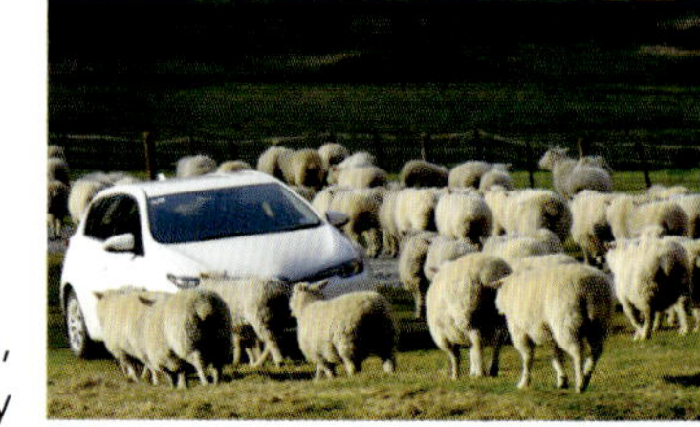

Droving sheep,
Matukituki Valley

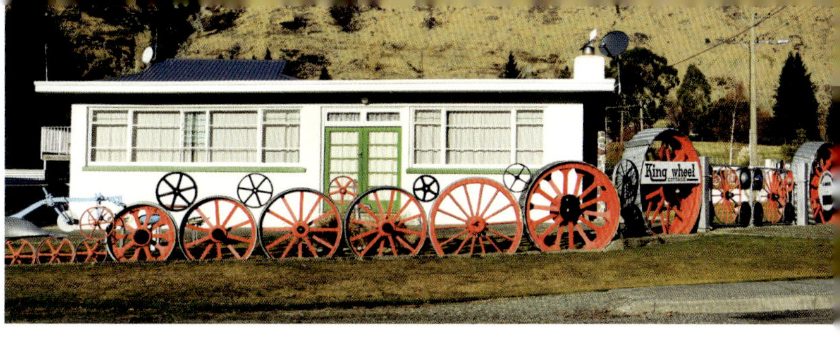

King Wheel Cottage, Kingston

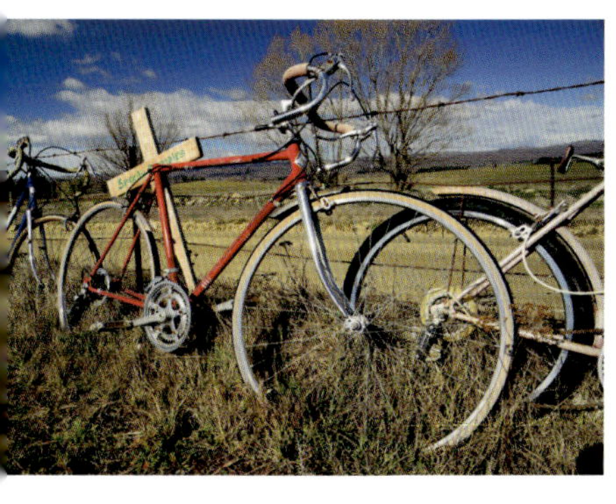
Bicycle fence, Alexandra

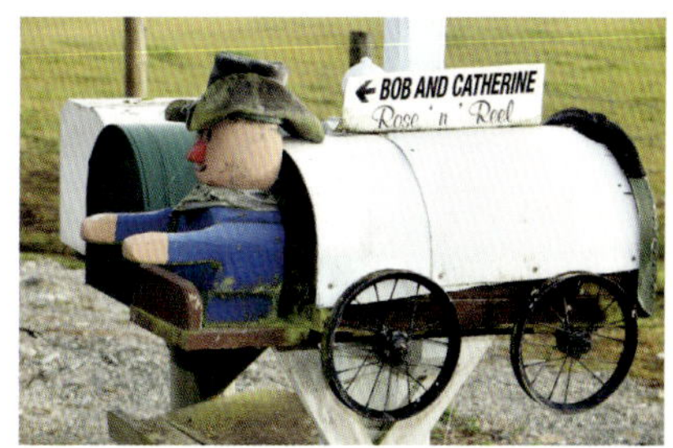

Farm letterbox near Te Anau

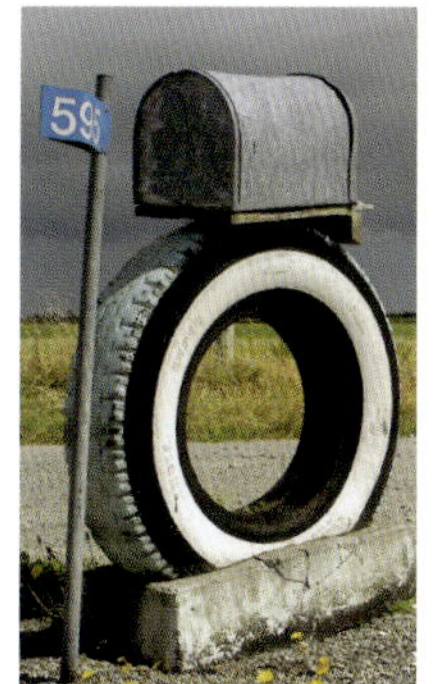
Letterbox near Clifden

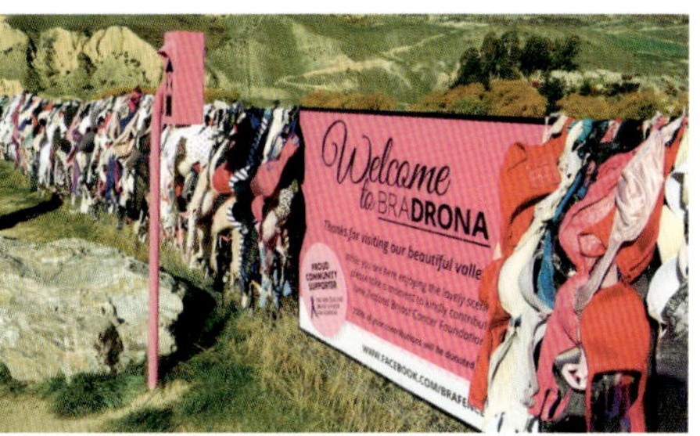

World-famous bra fence, Cardrona

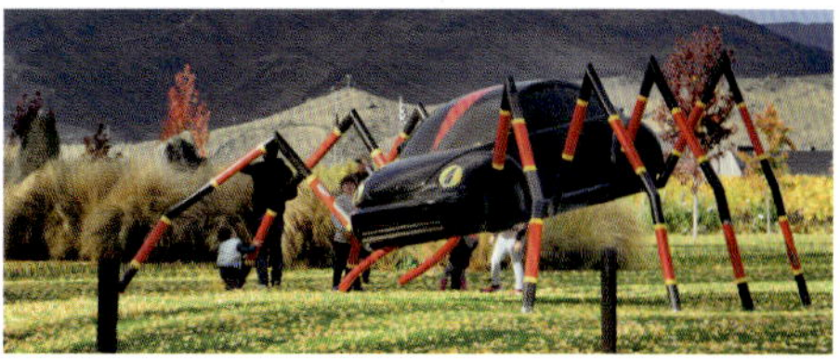
Car sculpture, Cromwell

Kawarau Gorge

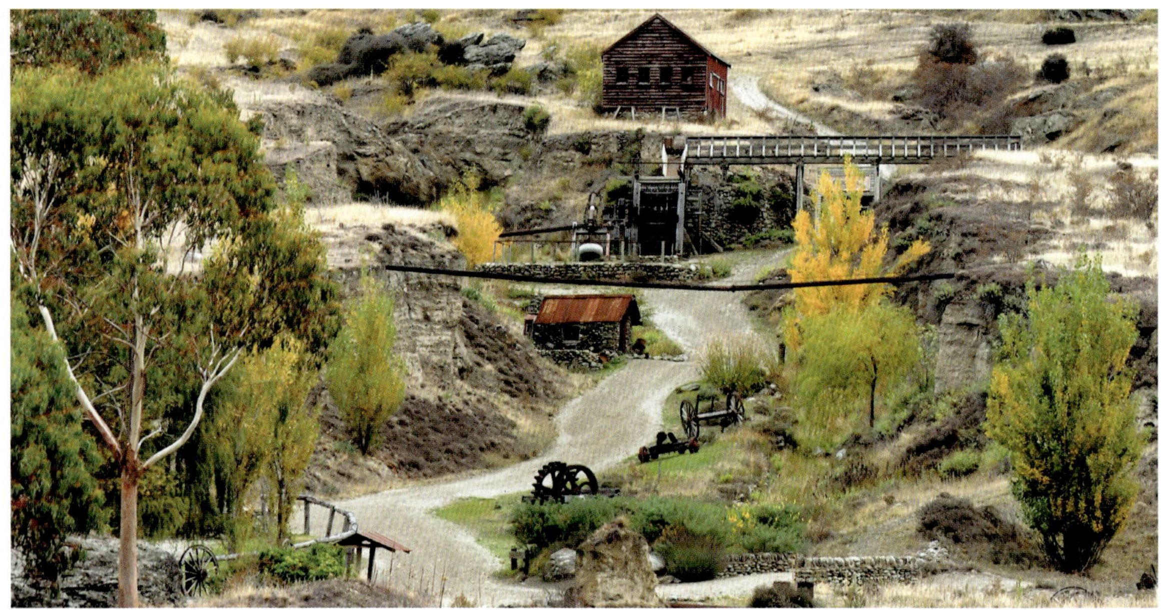

Goldfields Mining Centre

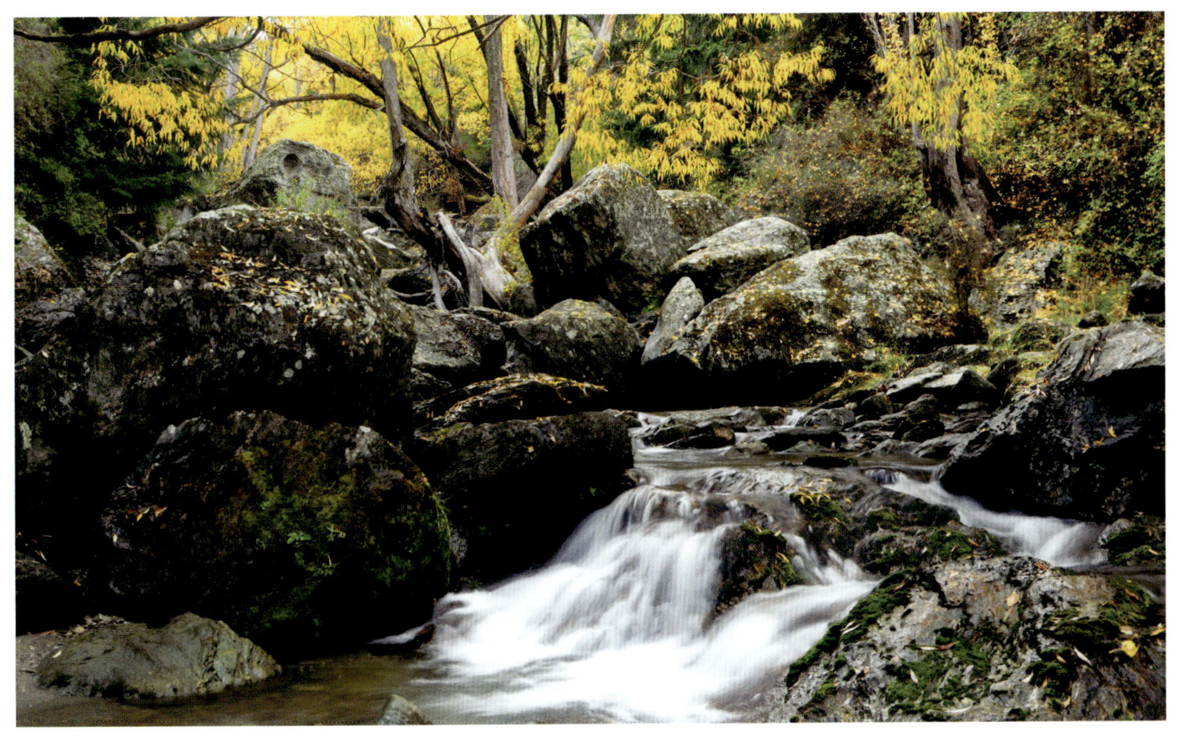

Roaring Meg Stream

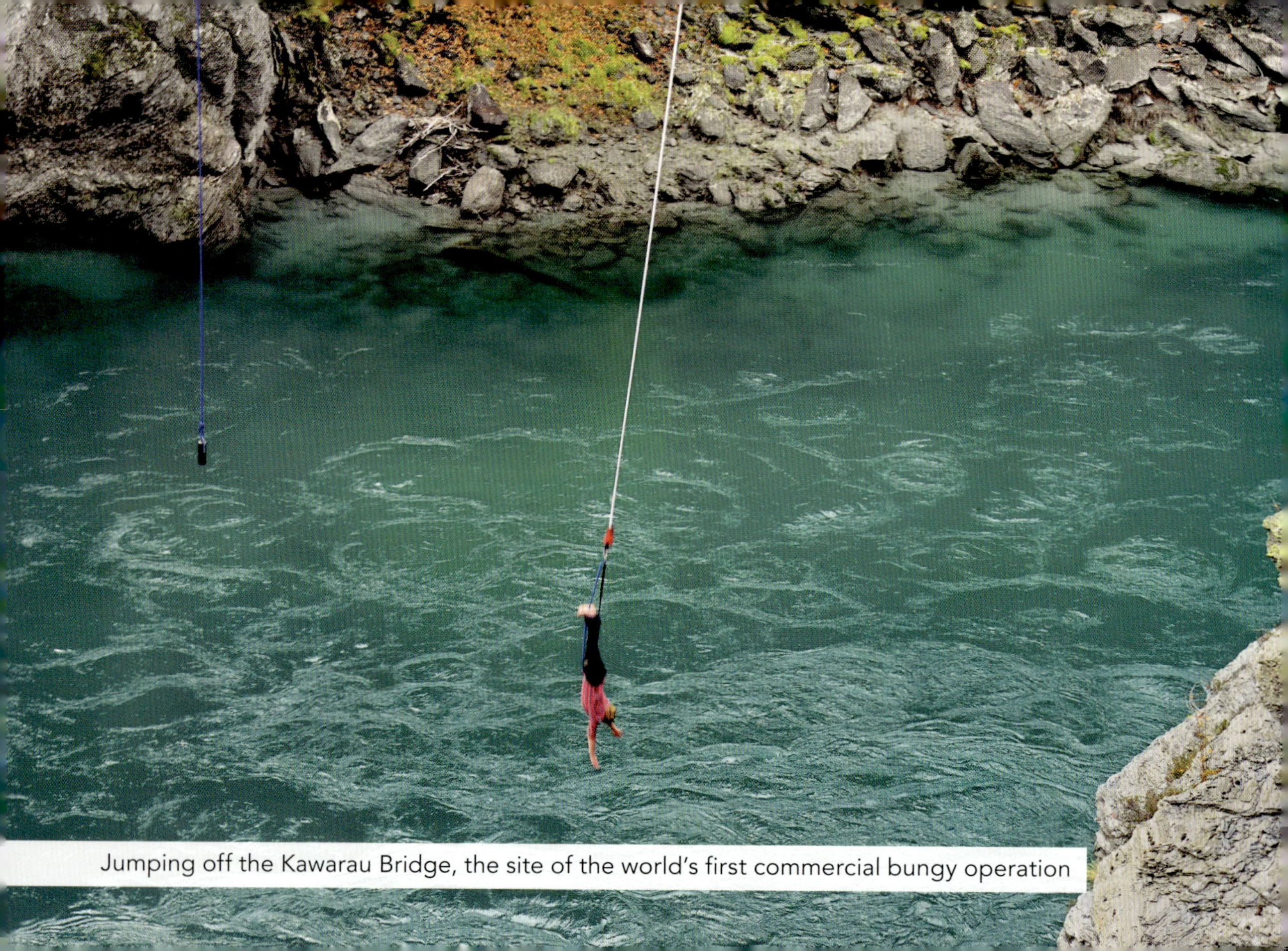

Jumping off the Kawarau Bridge, the site of the world's first commercial bungy operation

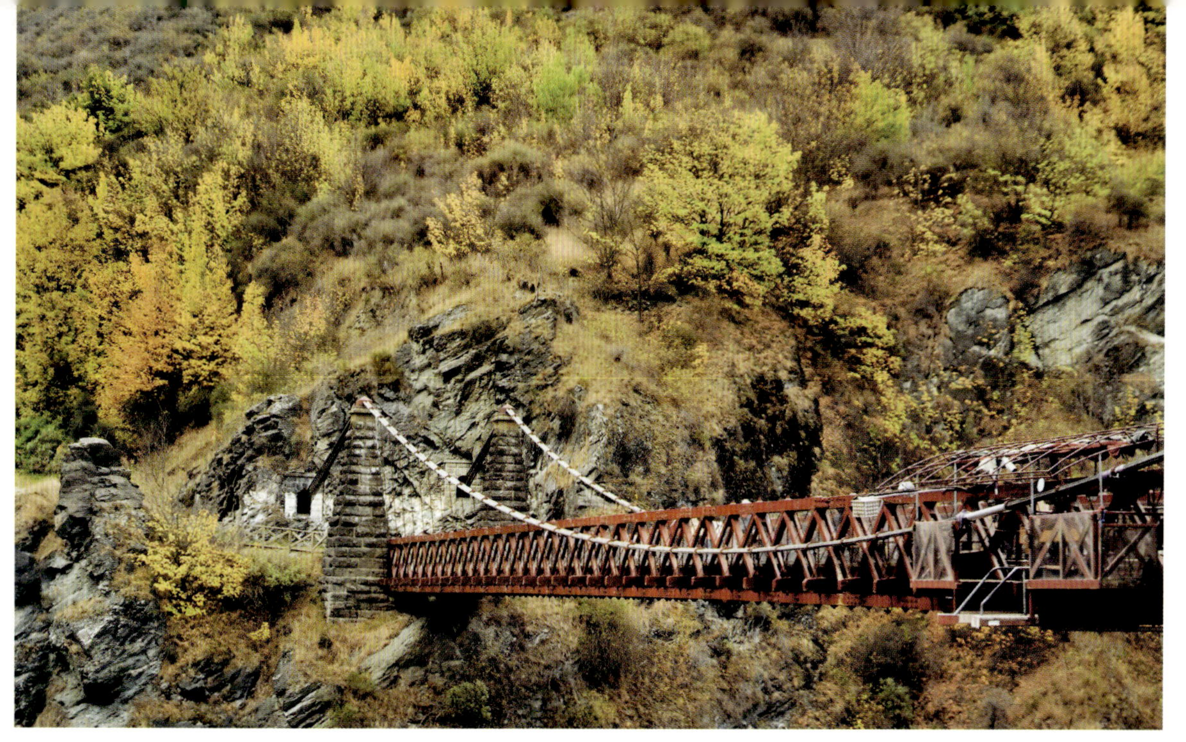

Historic suspension bridge over Kawarau River

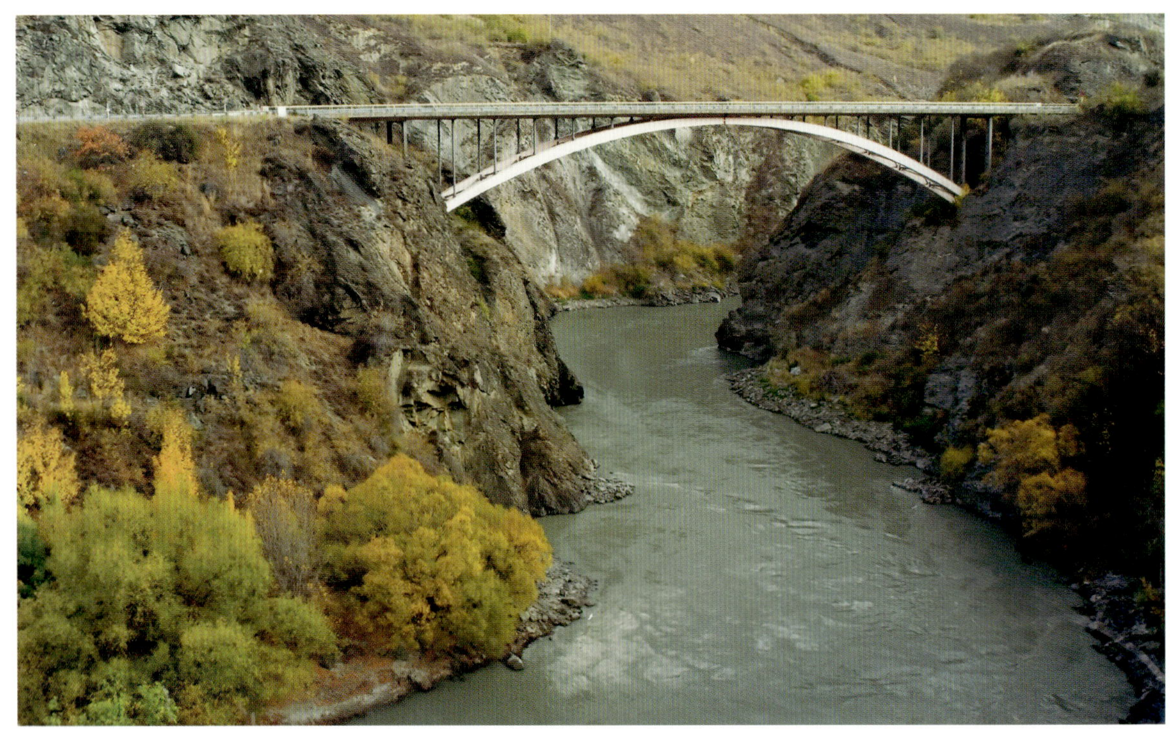

Kawarau Gorge

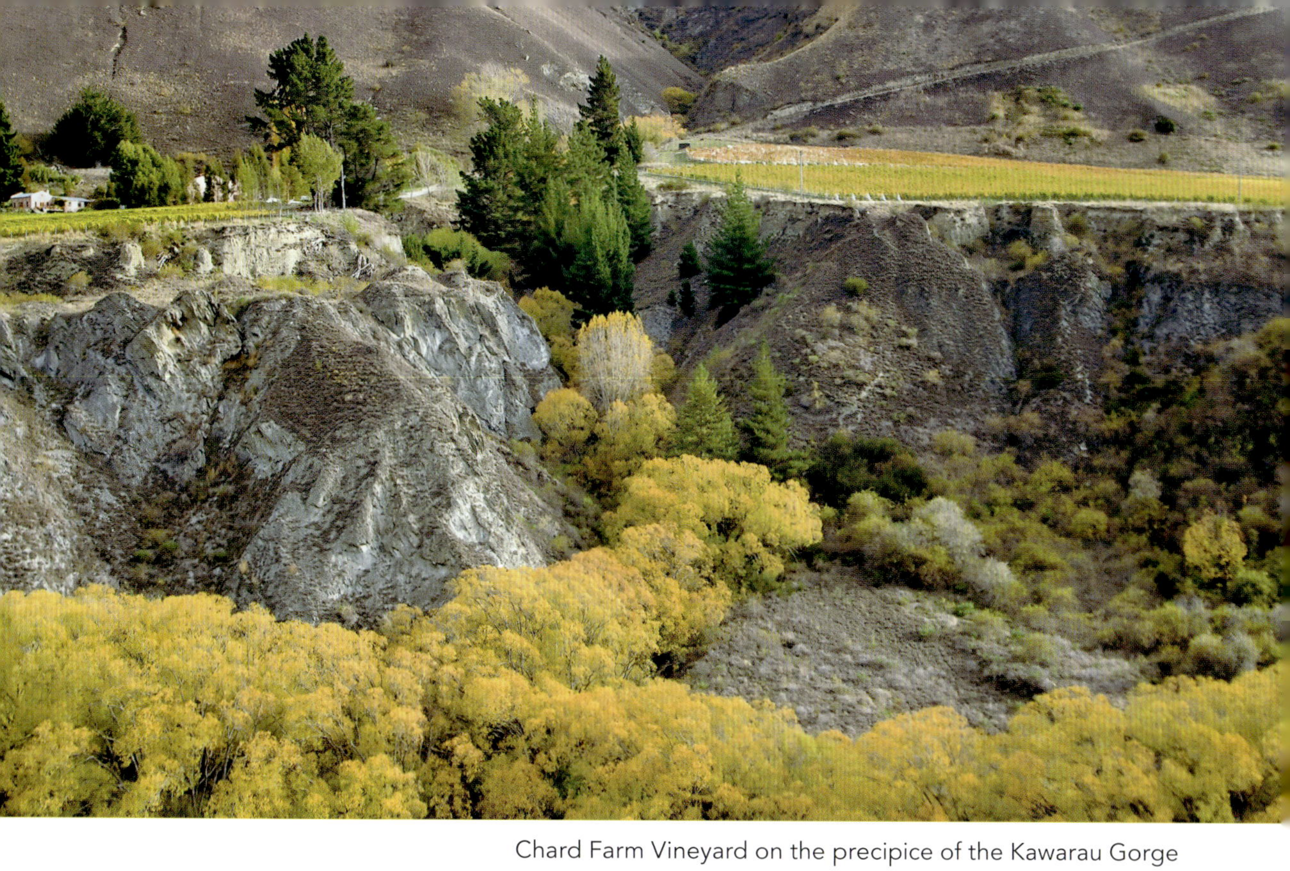

Chard Farm Vineyard on the precipice of the Kawarau Gorge

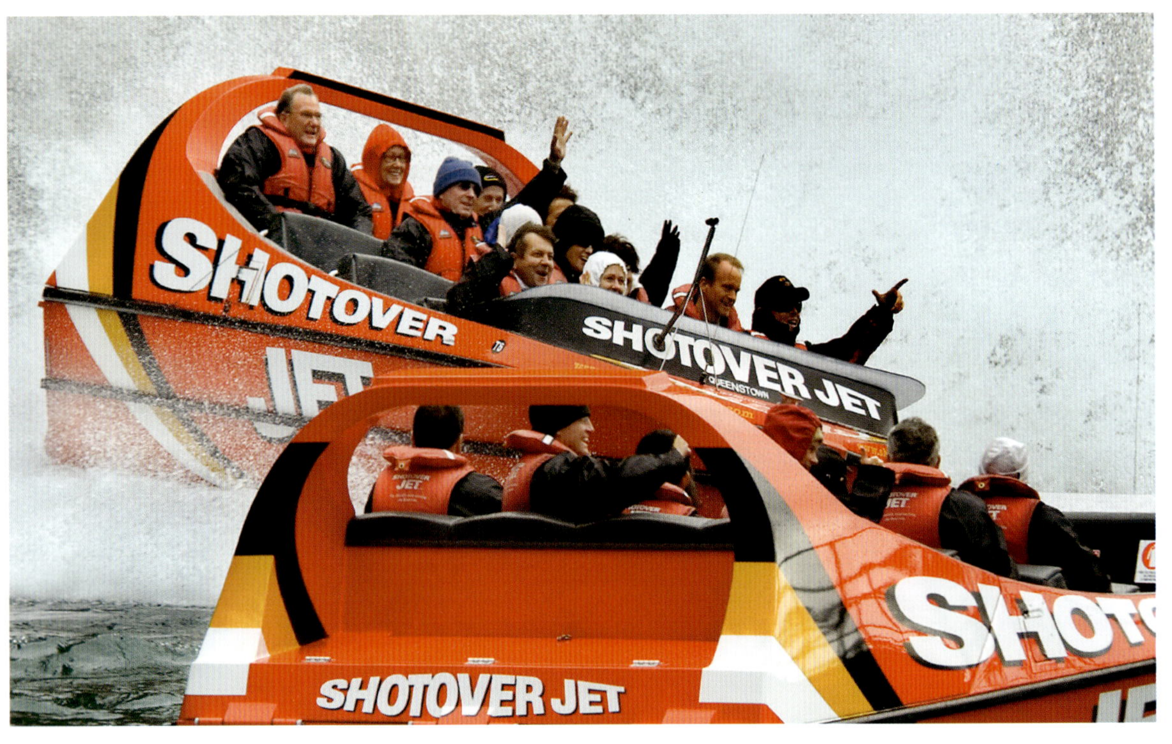
SHOTOVER
JET
SHOTOVER JET
QUEENSTOWN
SHOTOVER JET

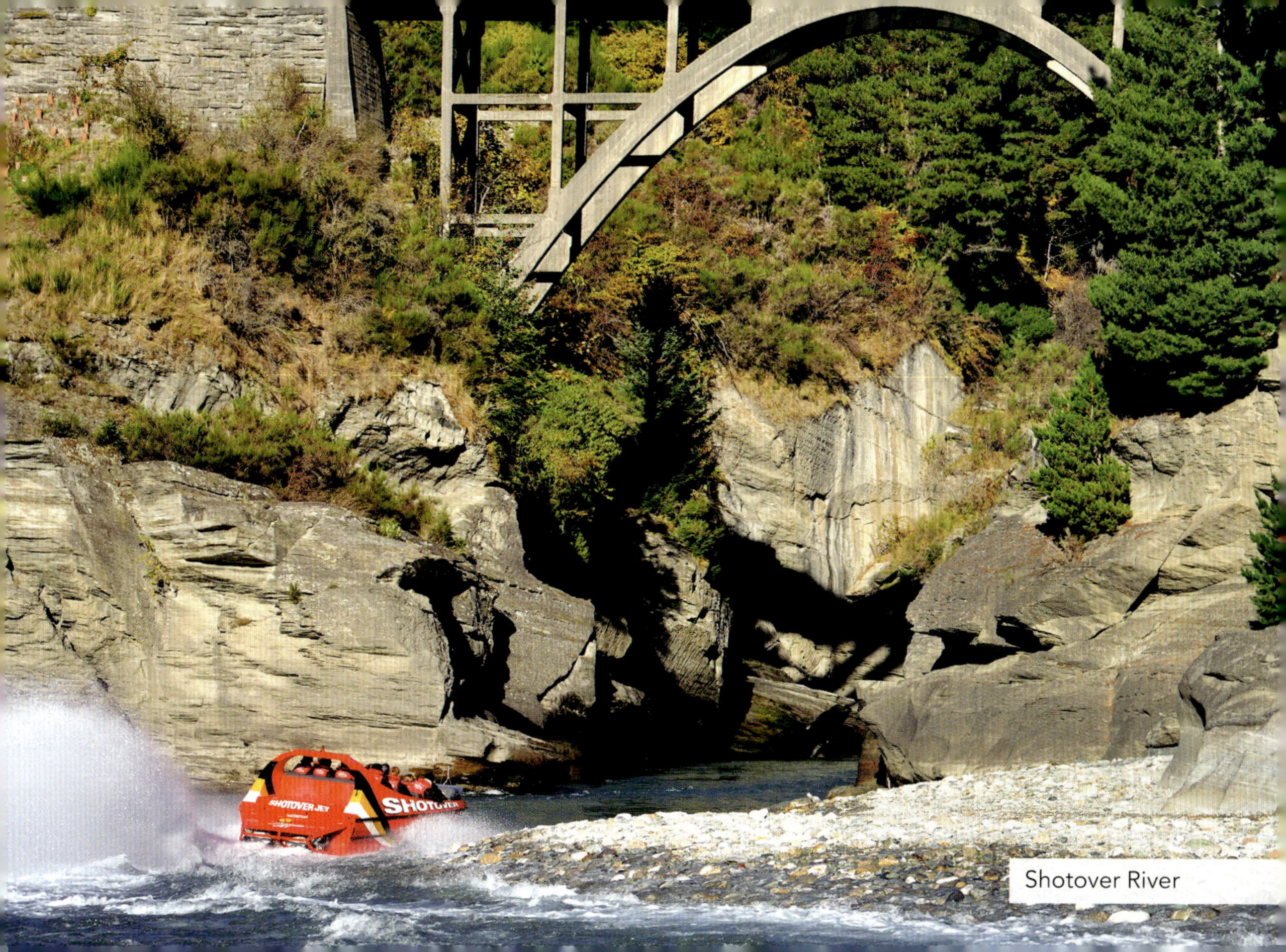

Shotover River

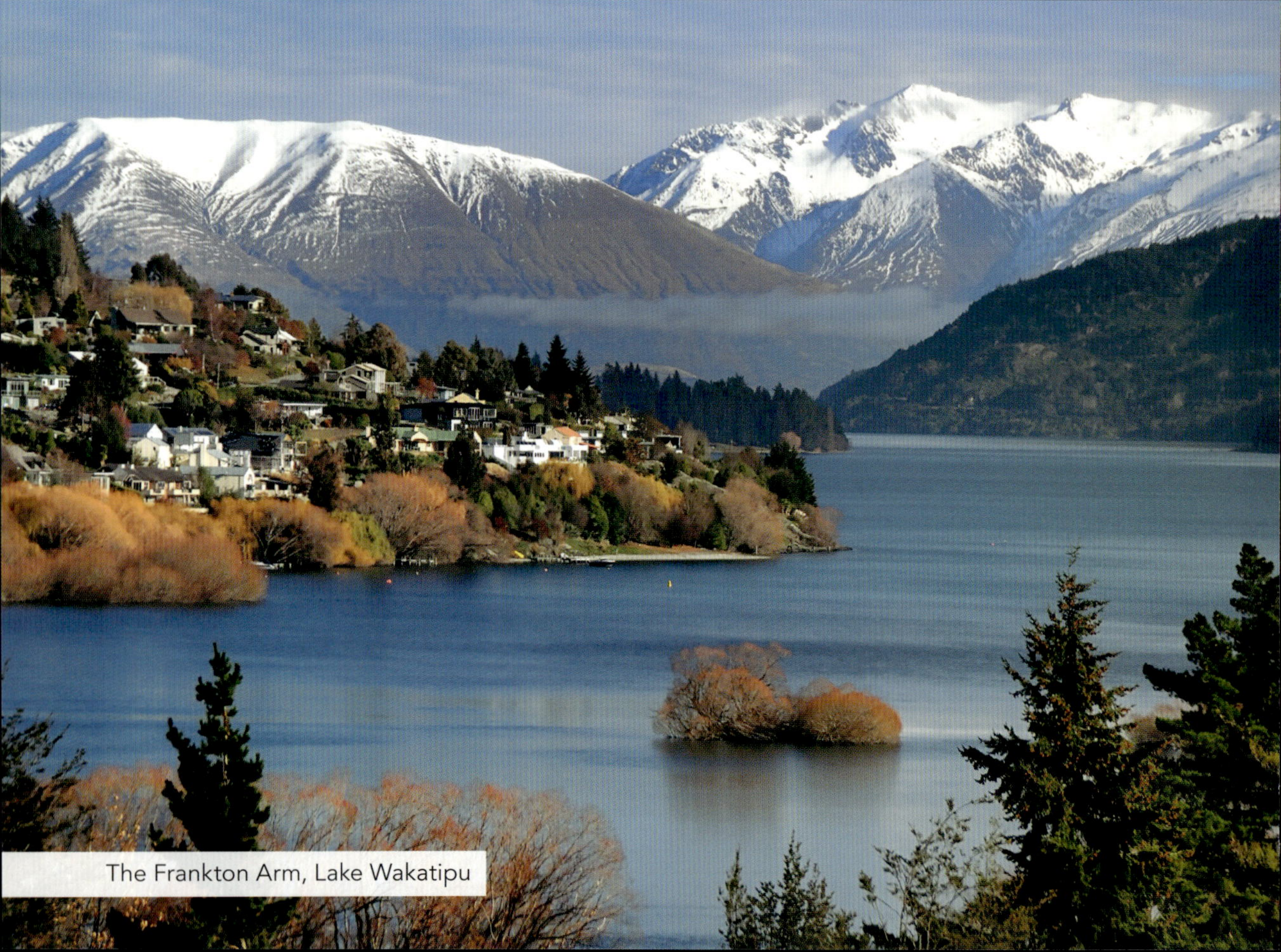

The Frankton Arm, Lake Wakatipu

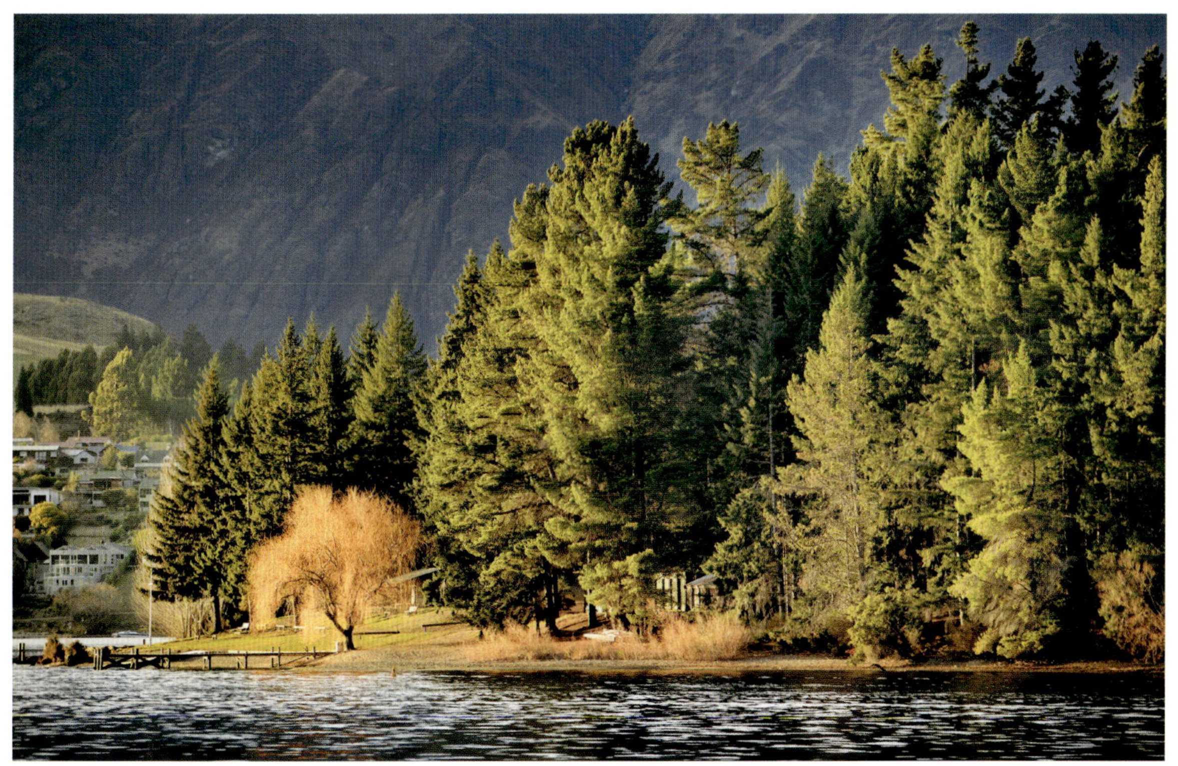

Lakeside, Kelvin Heights

The Remarkables Ski Field

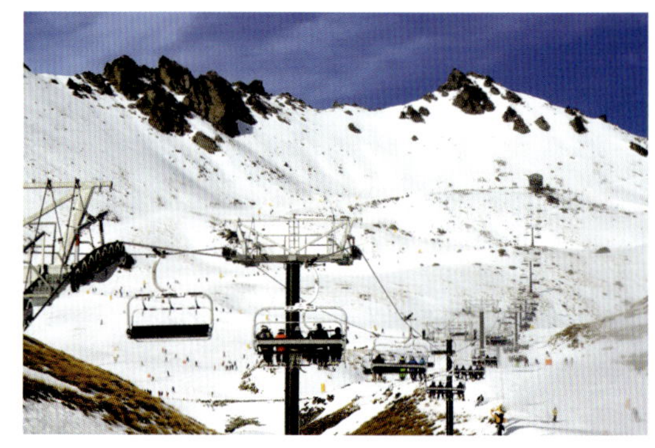

86

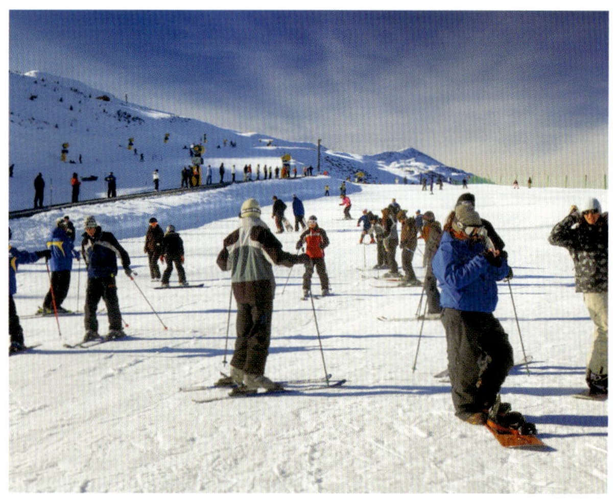

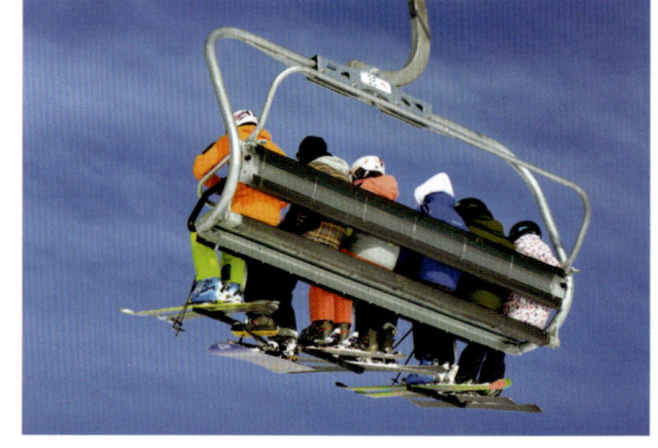

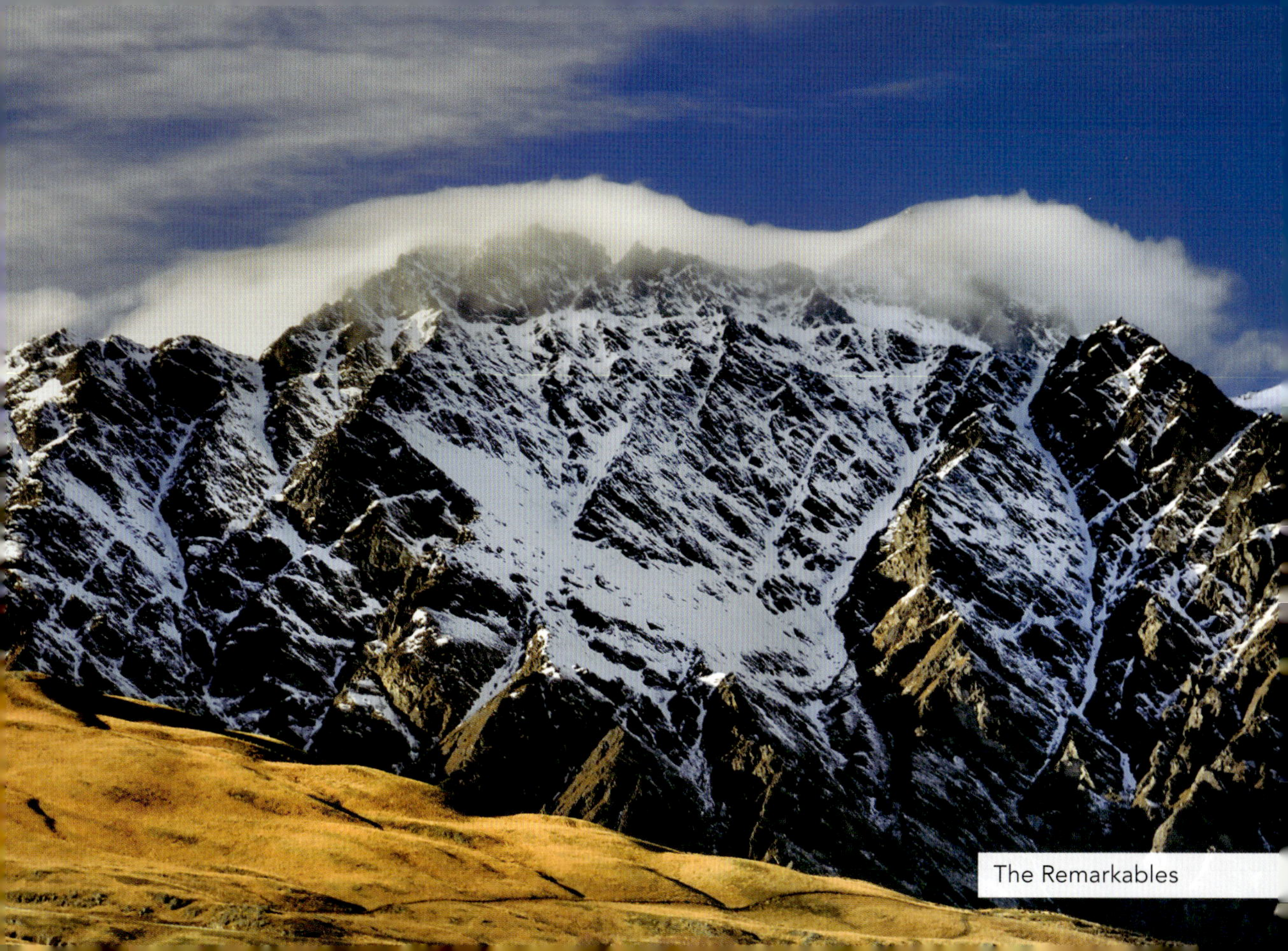

The Remarkables

Kingston to Te Waewae Bay

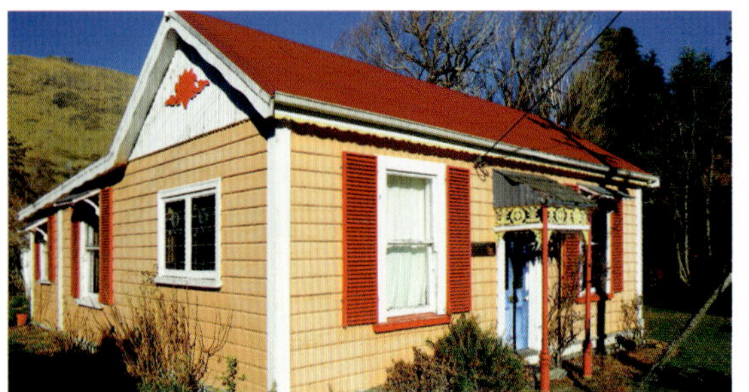

Restored cottage, Kingston

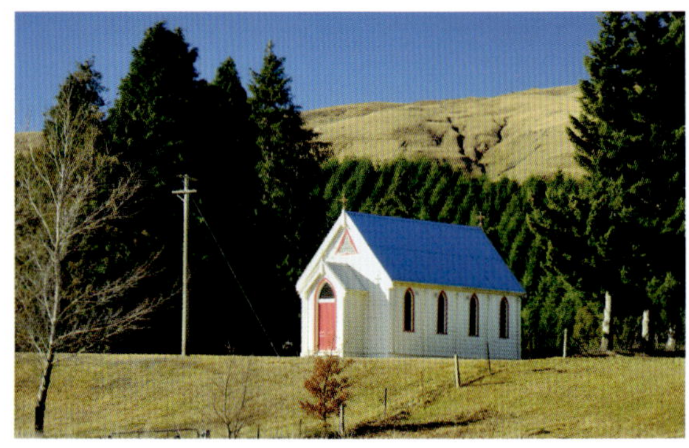

Country church, Garston

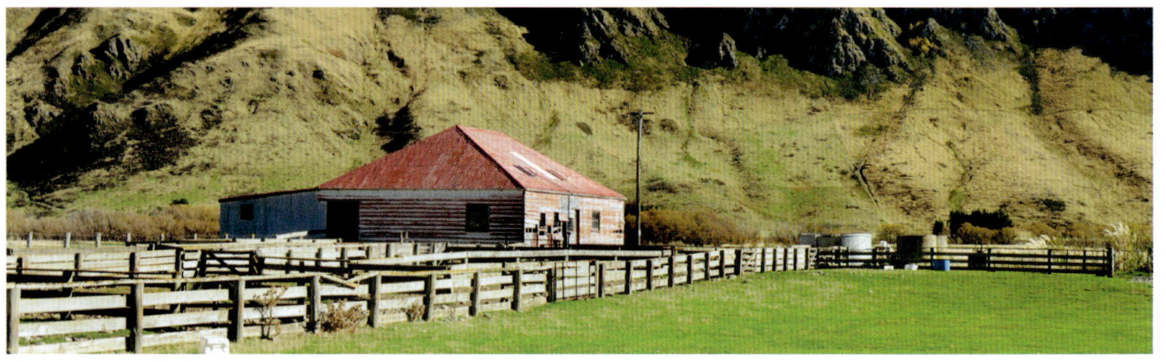

Farm near Athol

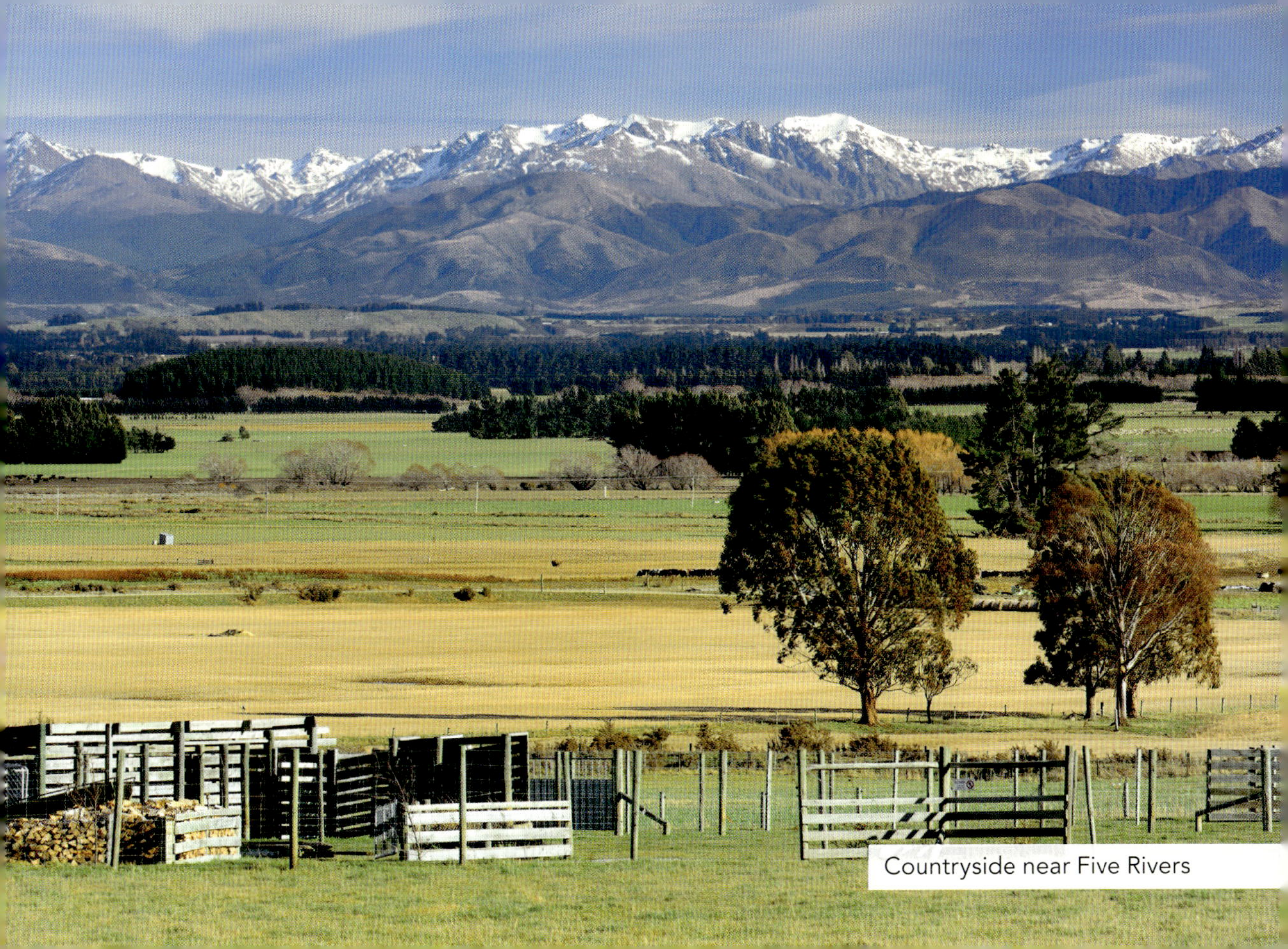

Countryside near Five Rivers

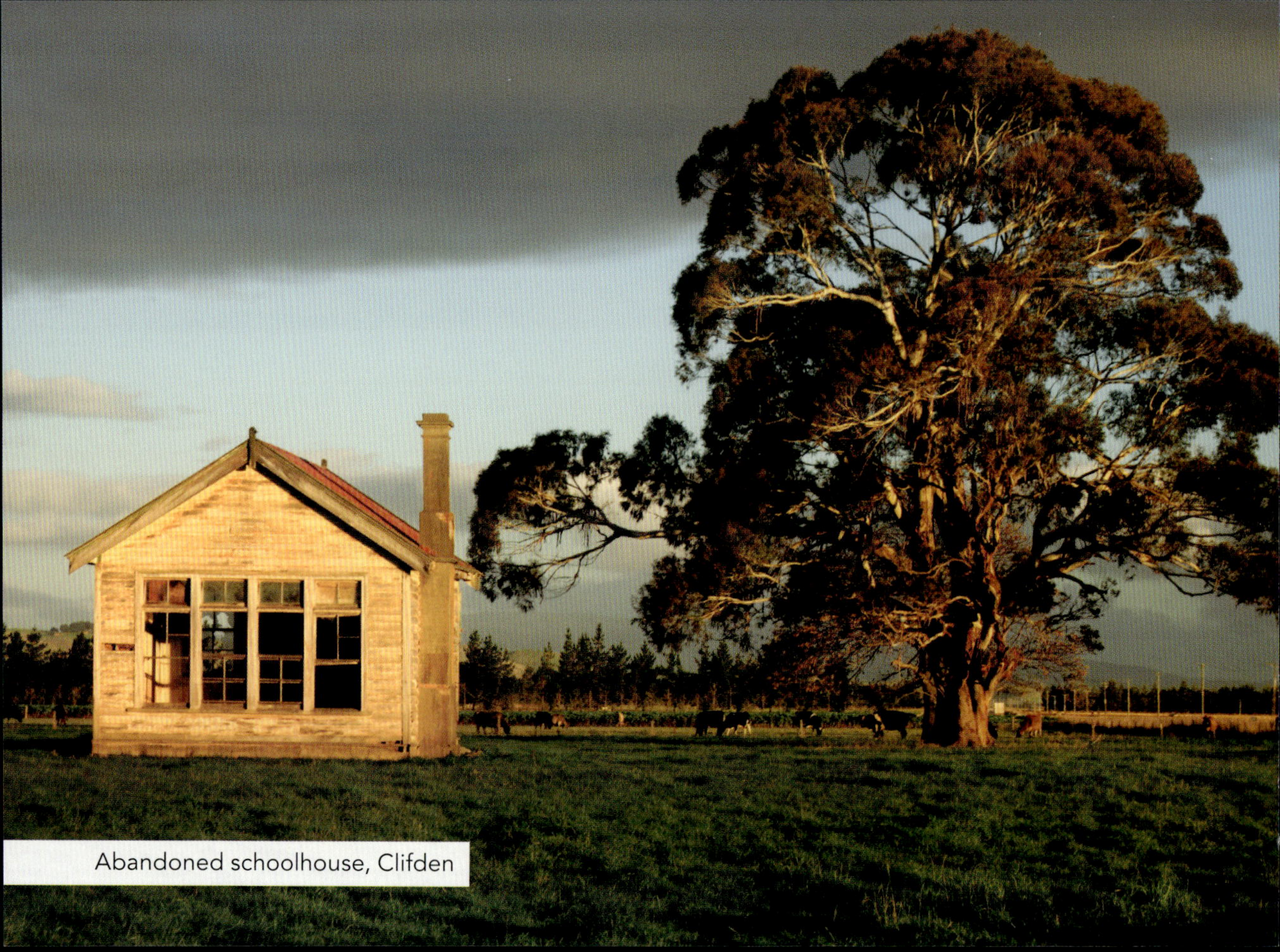

Abandoned schoolhouse, Clifden

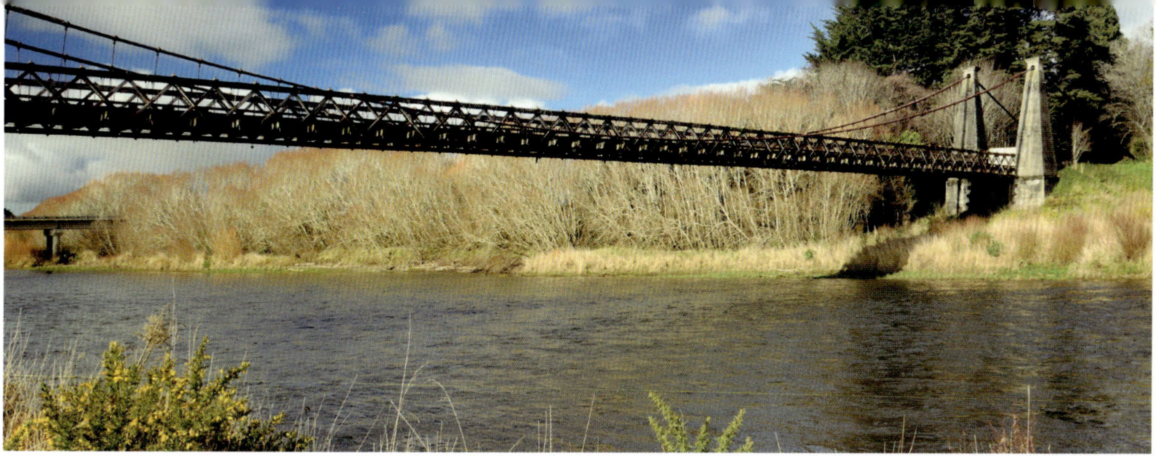

Historic Clifden Suspension Bridge over the Waiau River

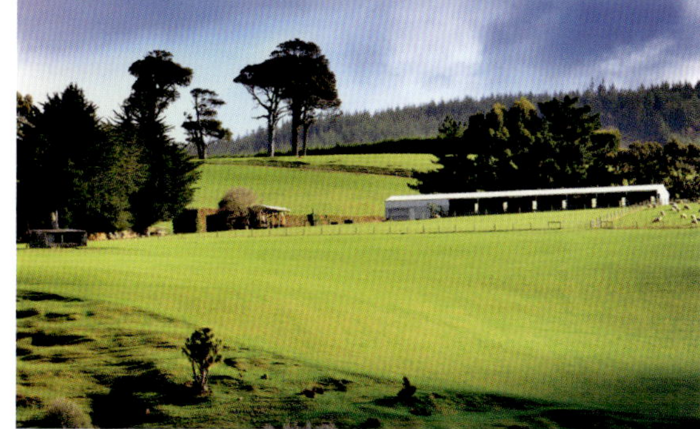

Countryside near Clifden

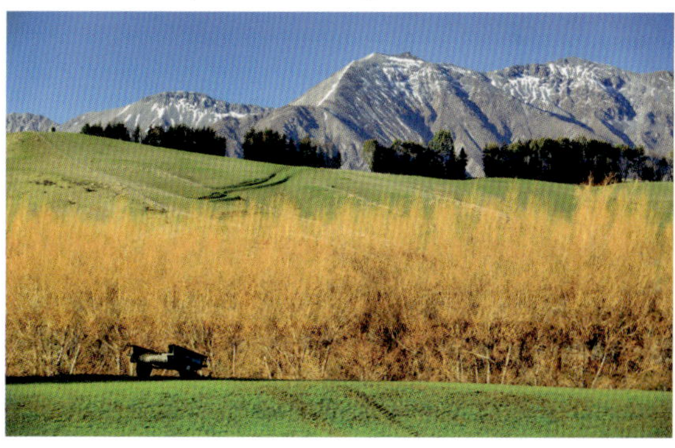

Takitimu Mountains near Manapouri

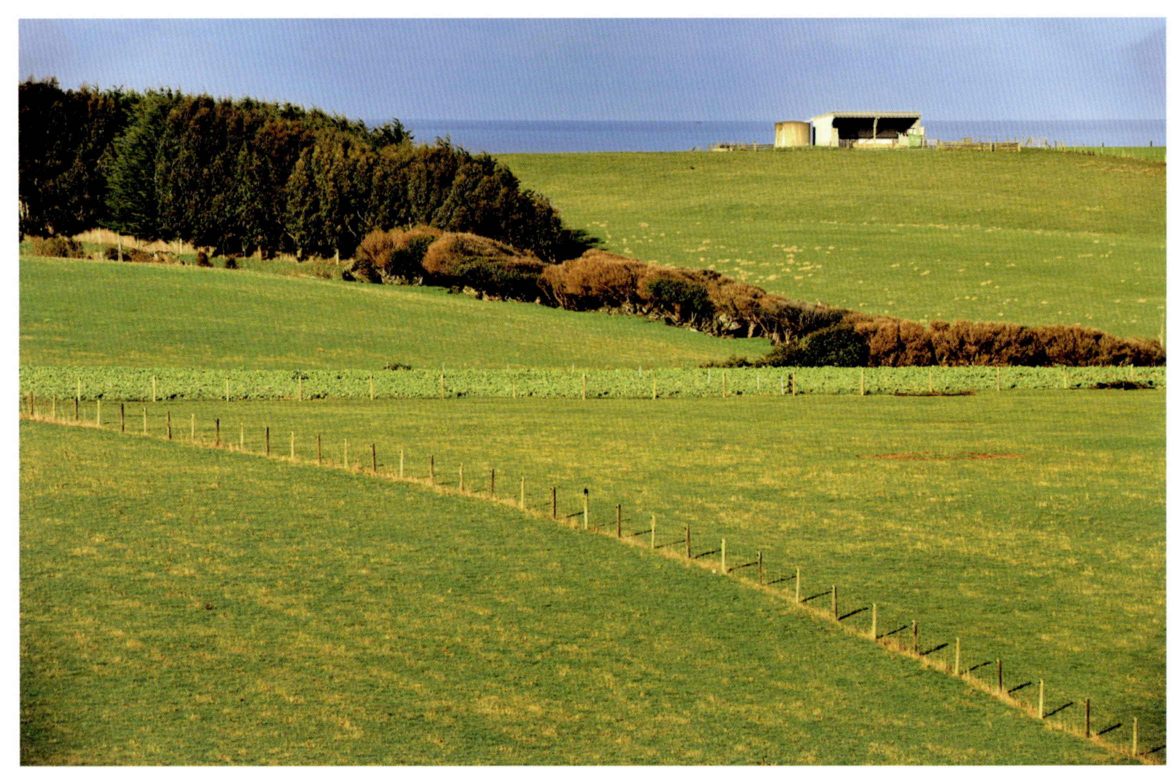

Farmland, Papatotara Coast Road

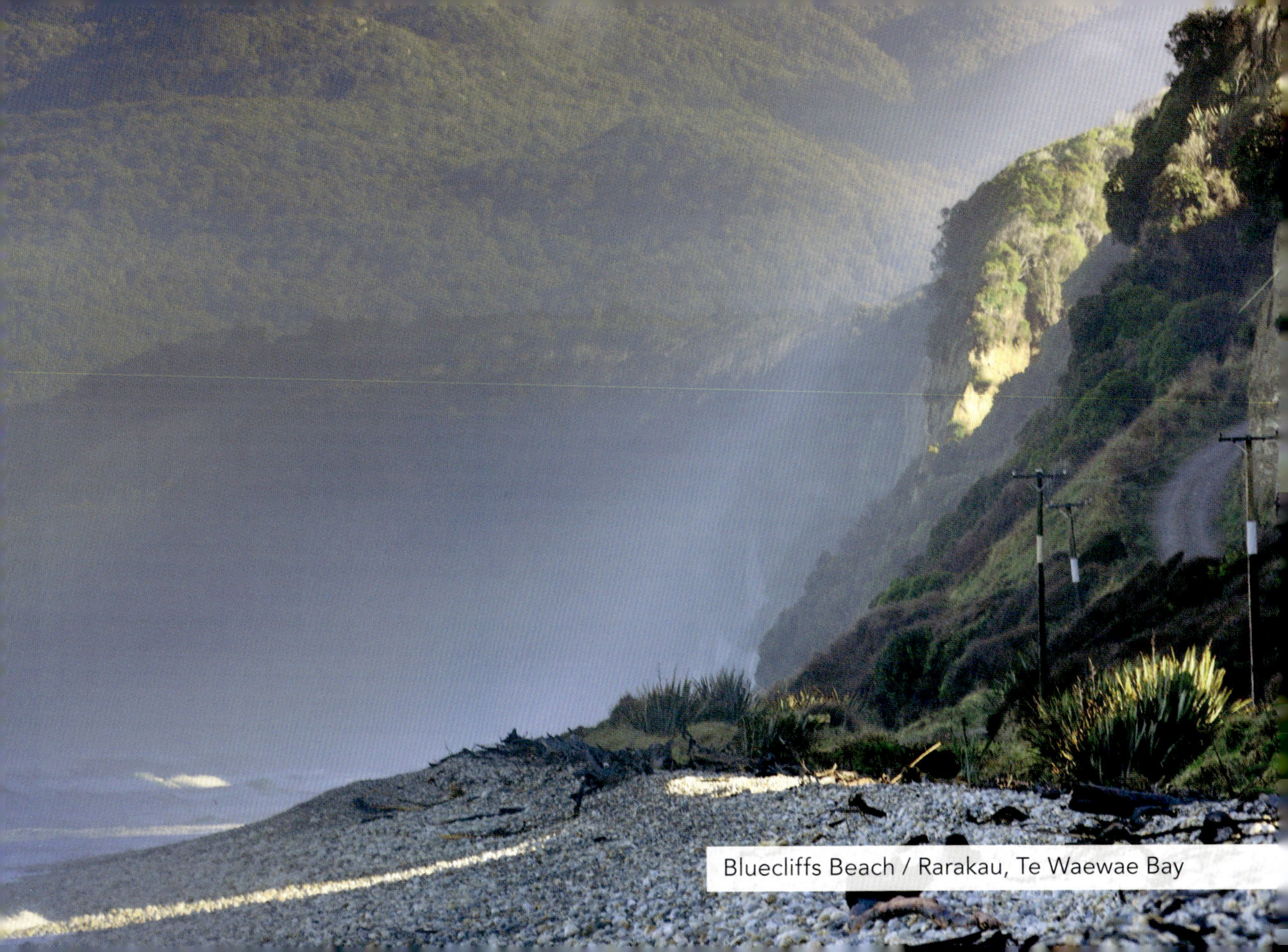

Bluecliffs Beach / Rarakau, Te Waewae Bay

Hydro Power Stations

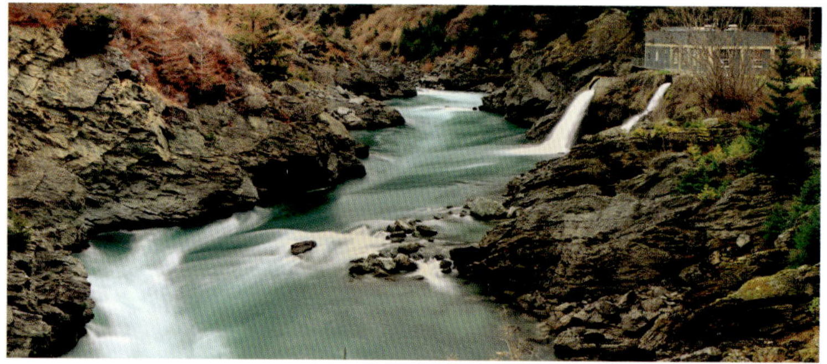

Roaring Meg power station, Kawarau Gorge

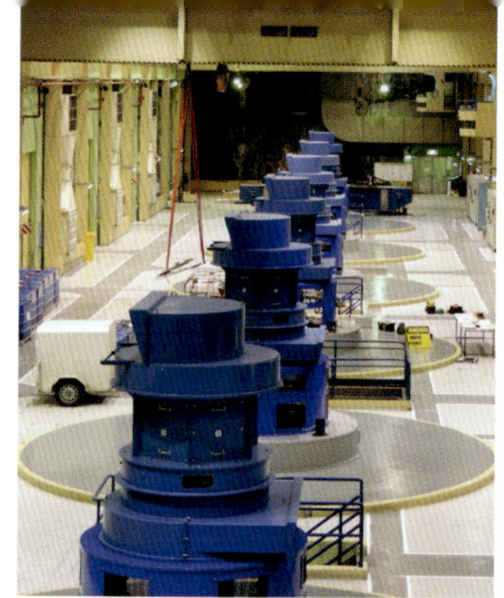

Turbines, Manapouri underground power station

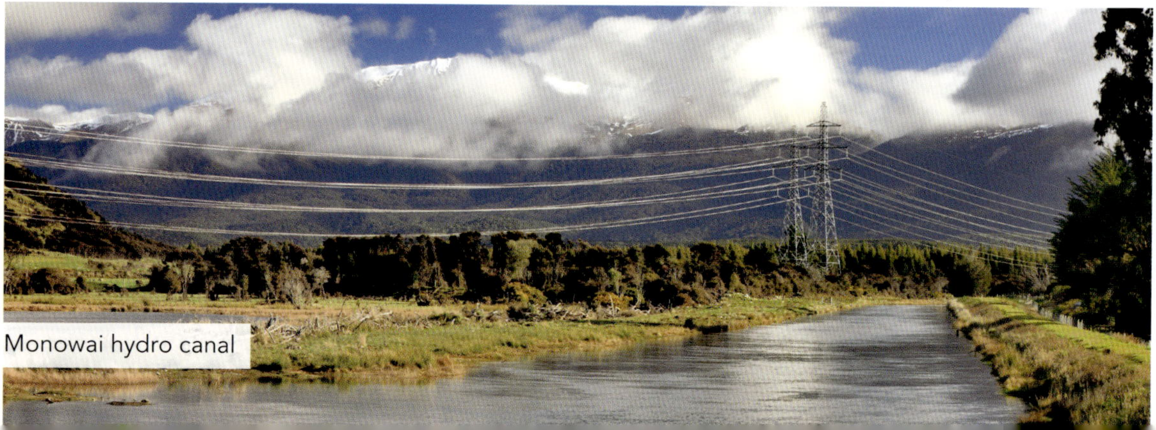

Monowai hydro canal

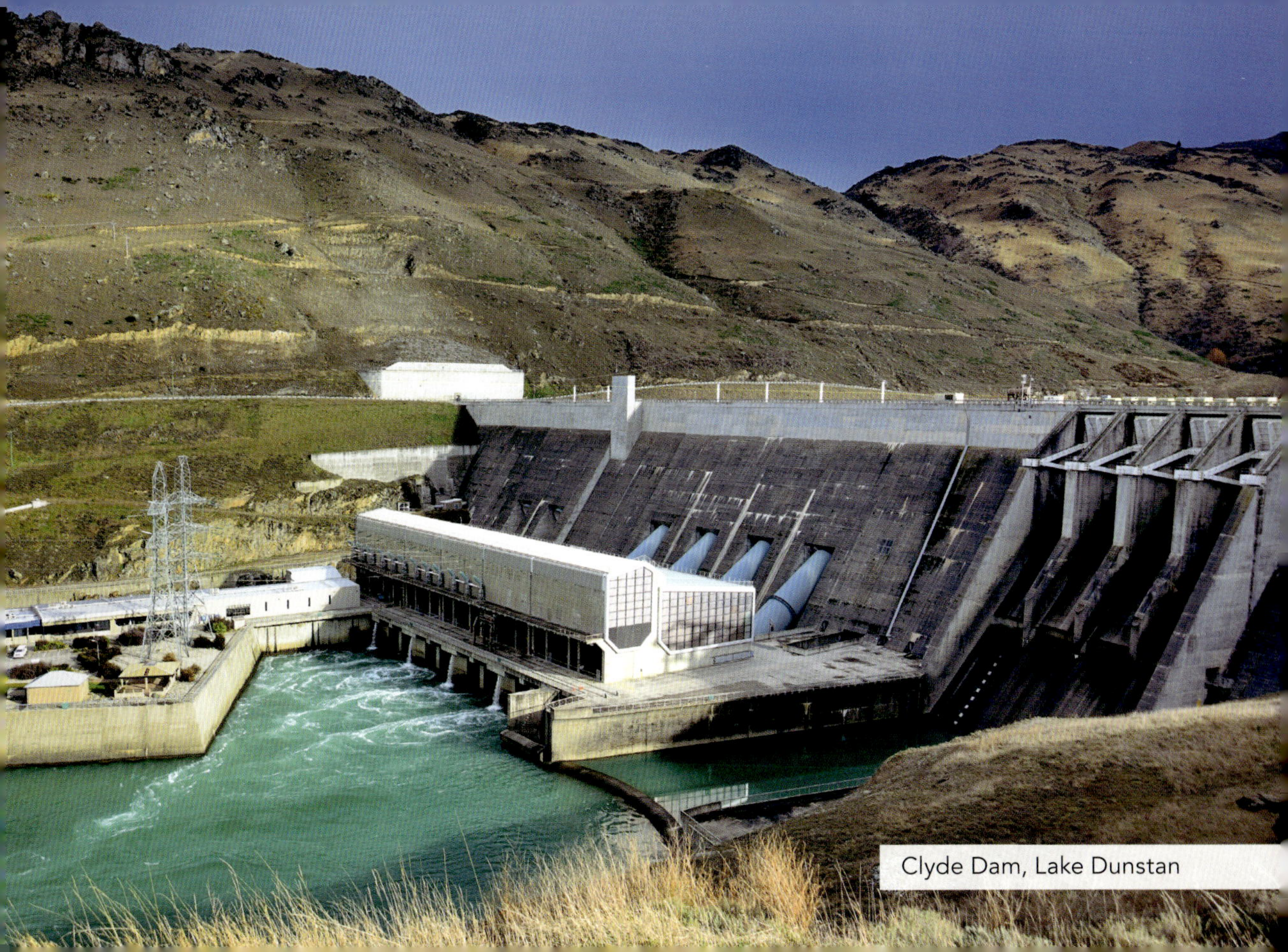
Clyde Dam, Lake Dunstan

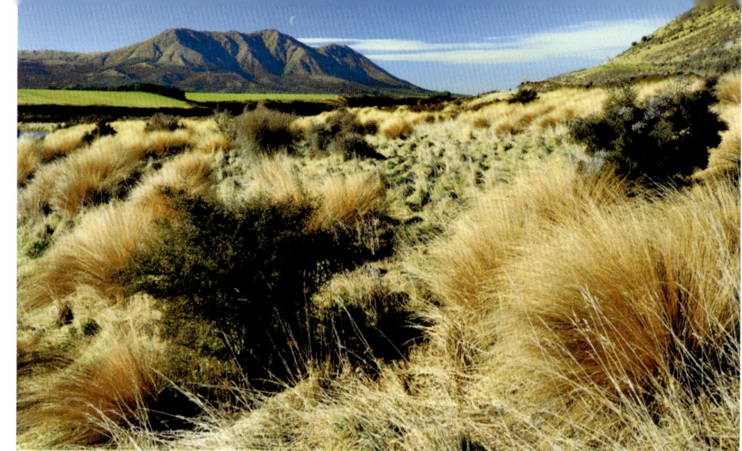

Te Anau basin

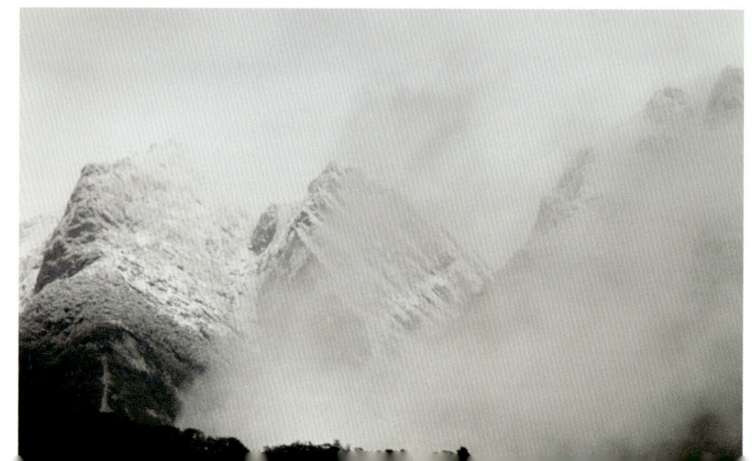

Misty mountains near Lake Manapouri

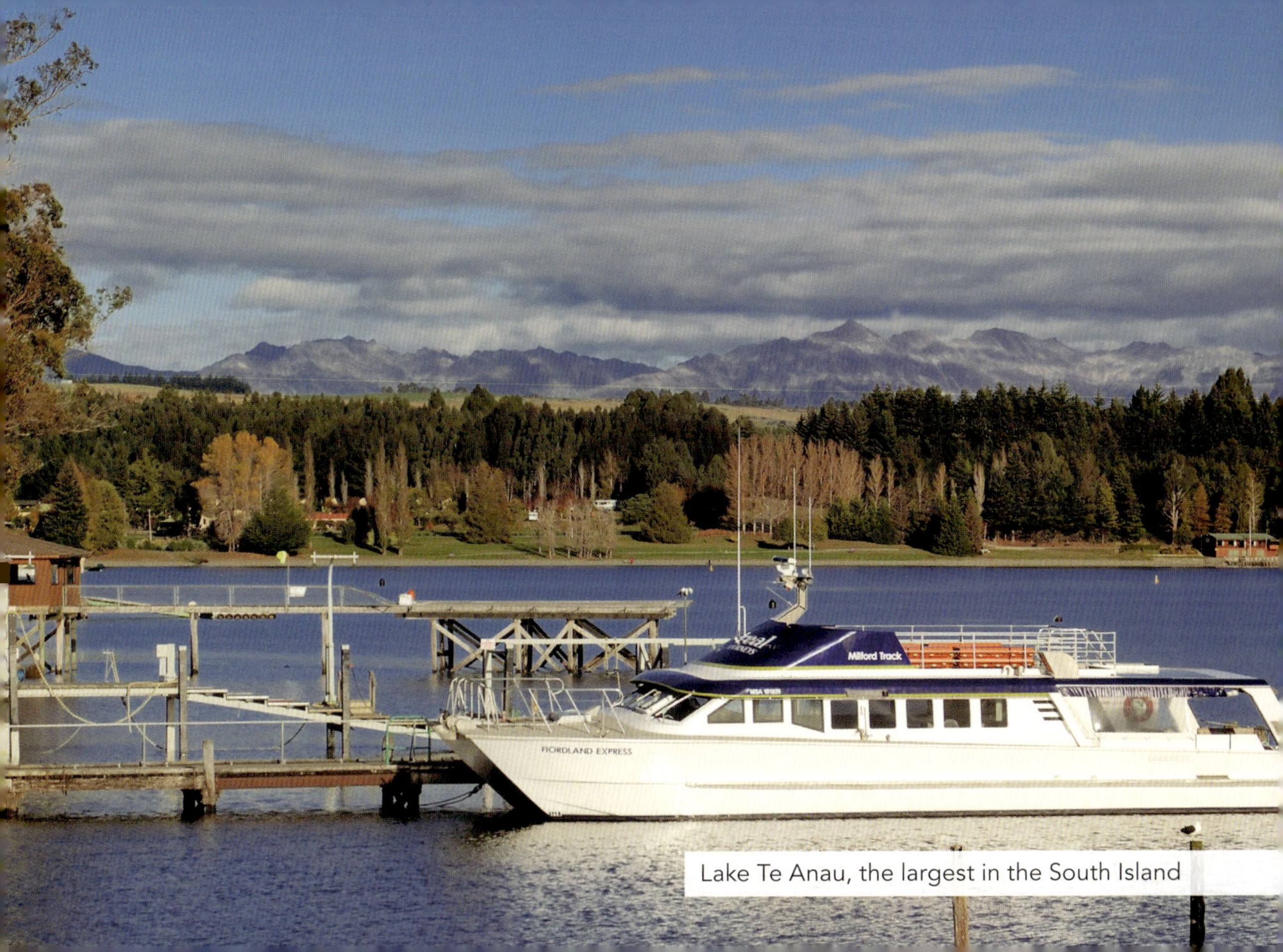

Lake Te Anau, the largest in the South Island

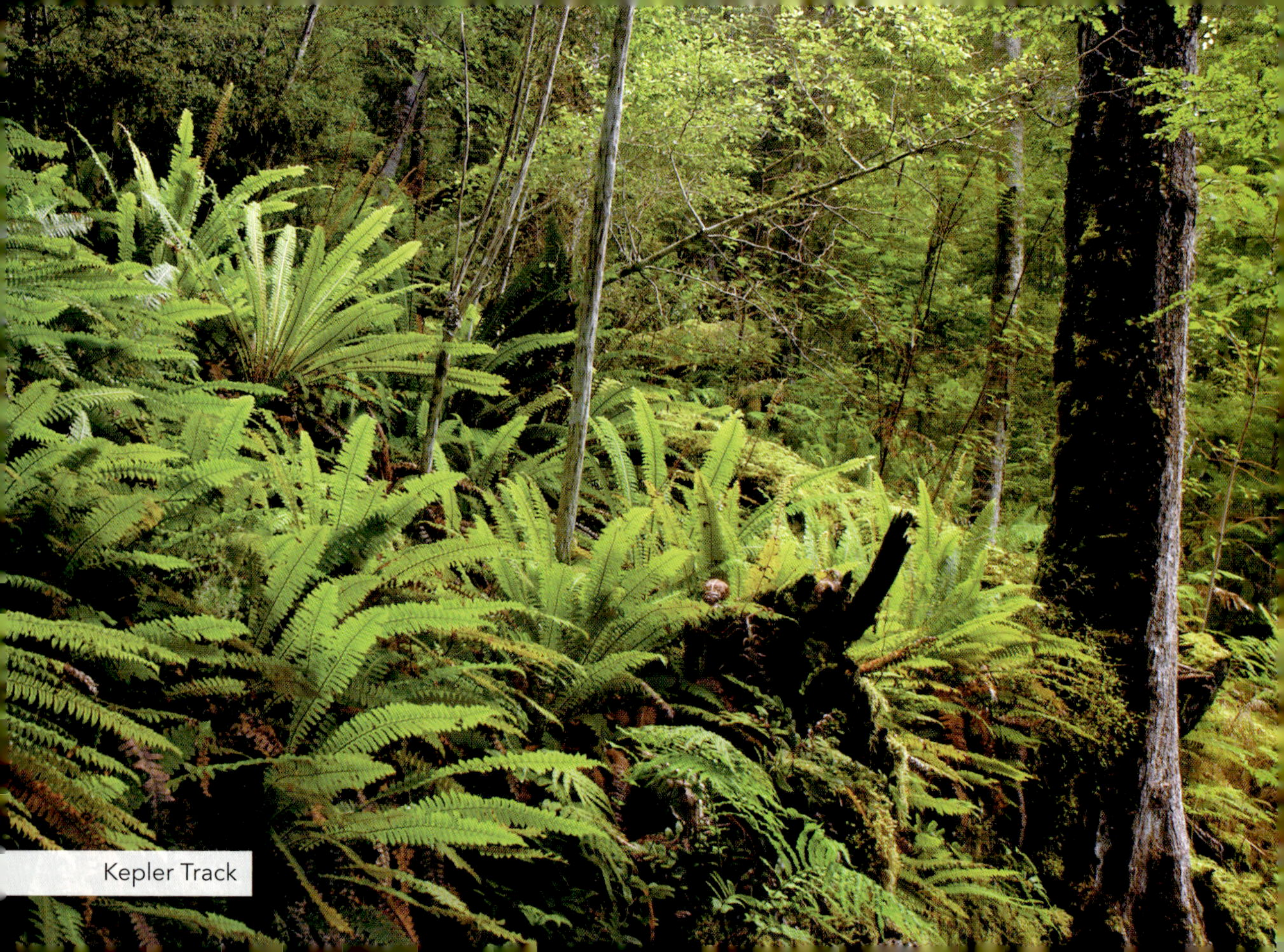

Kepler Track

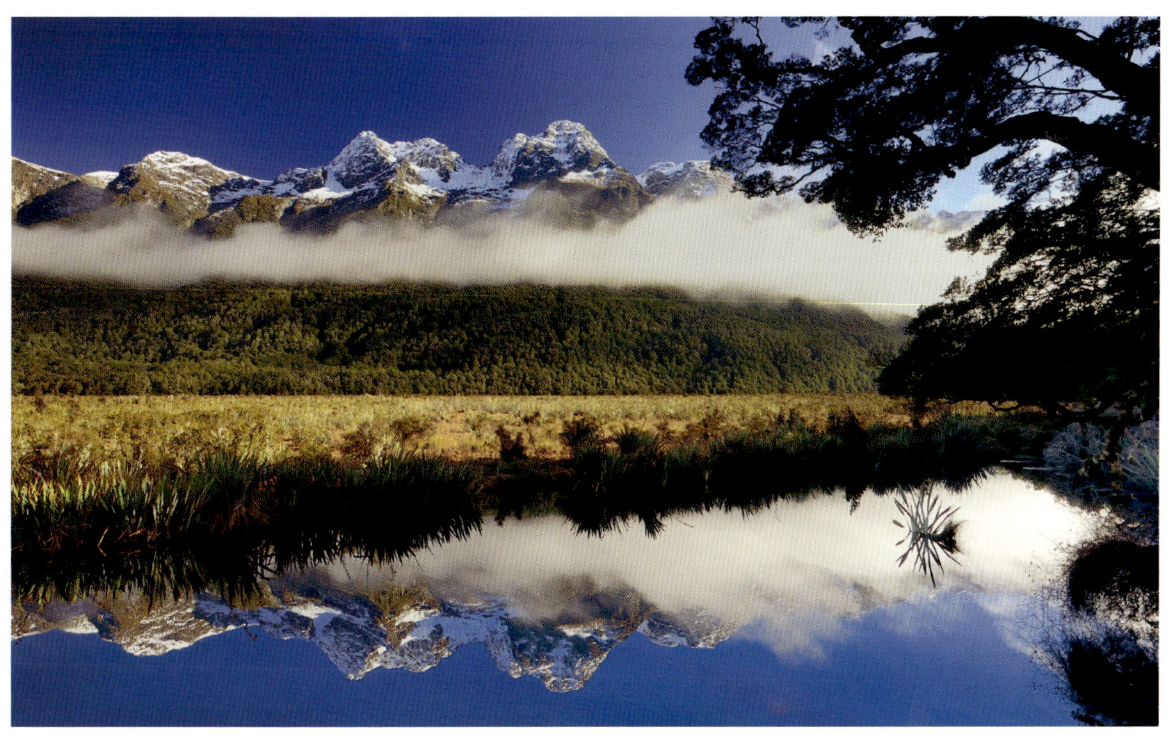

Mirror Lakes, Milford Road

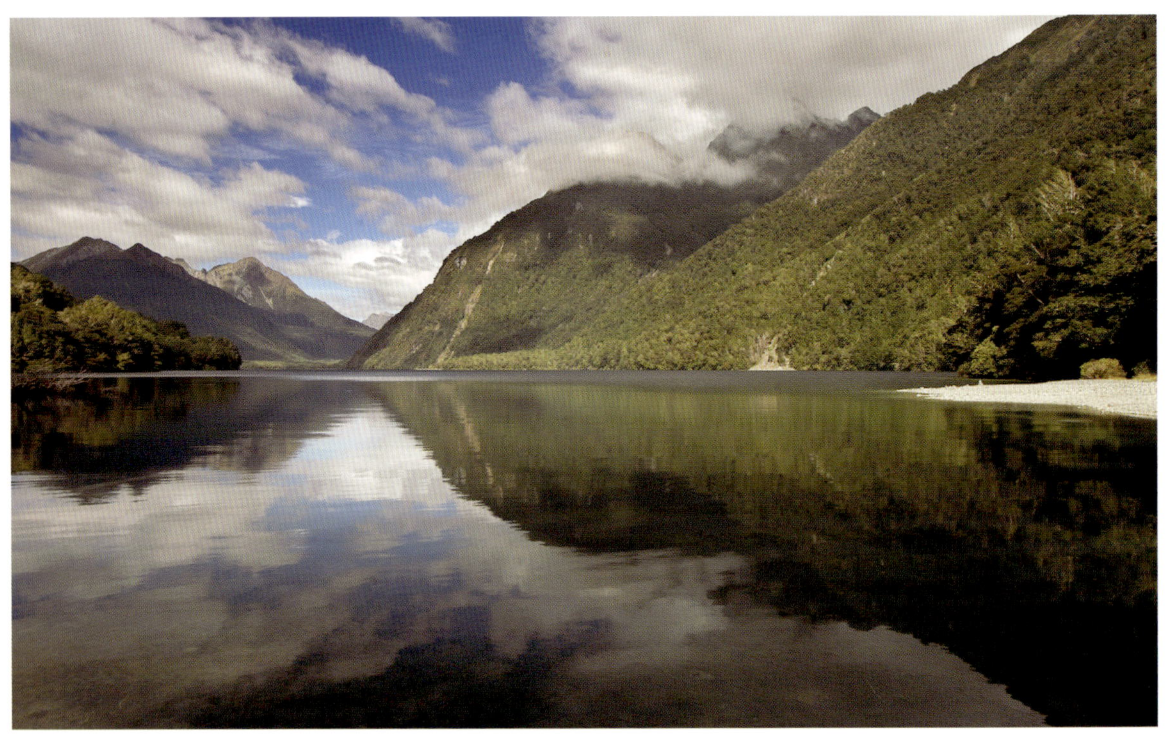

Lake Gunn

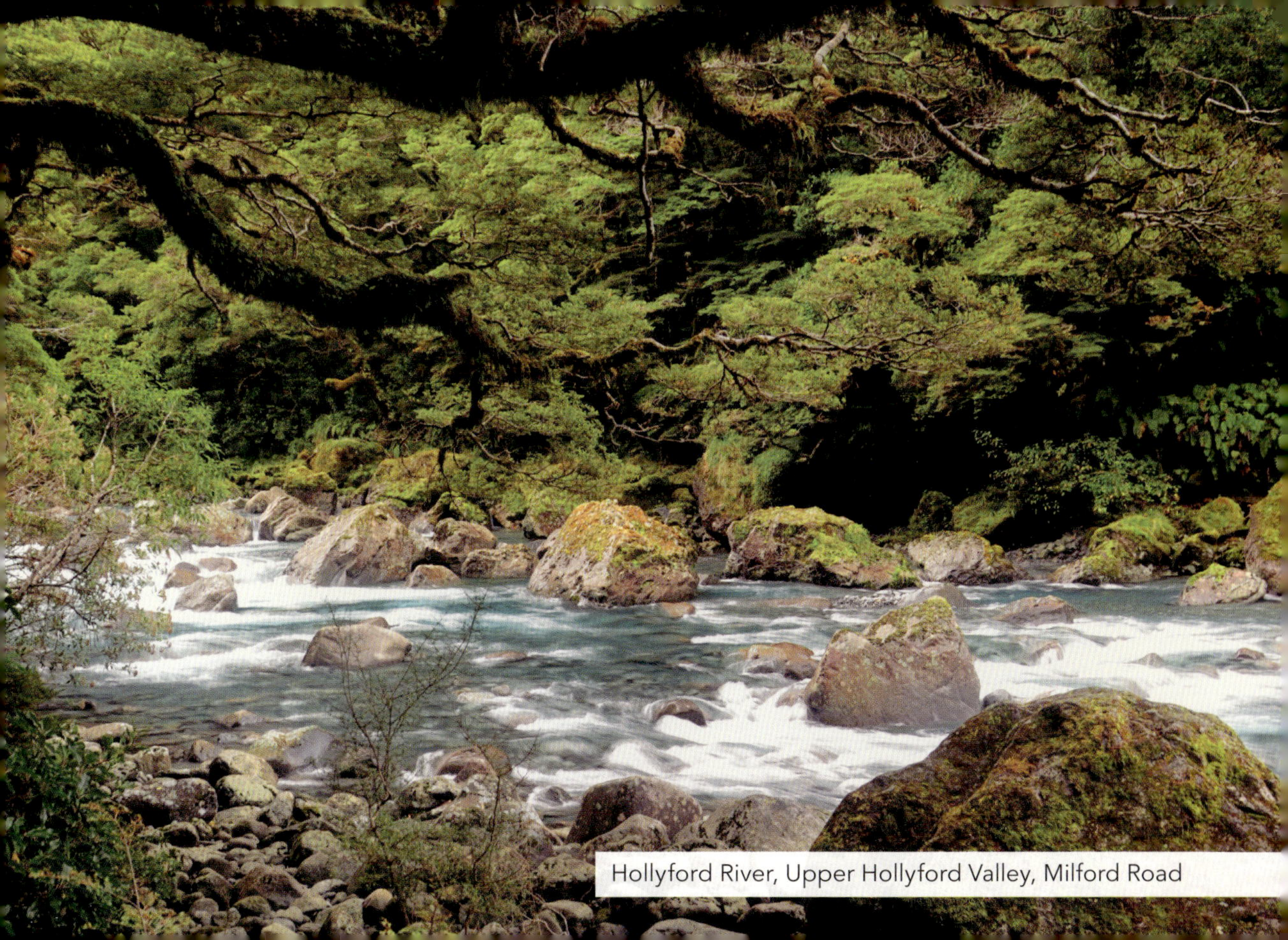

Hollyford River, Upper Hollyford Valley, Milford Road

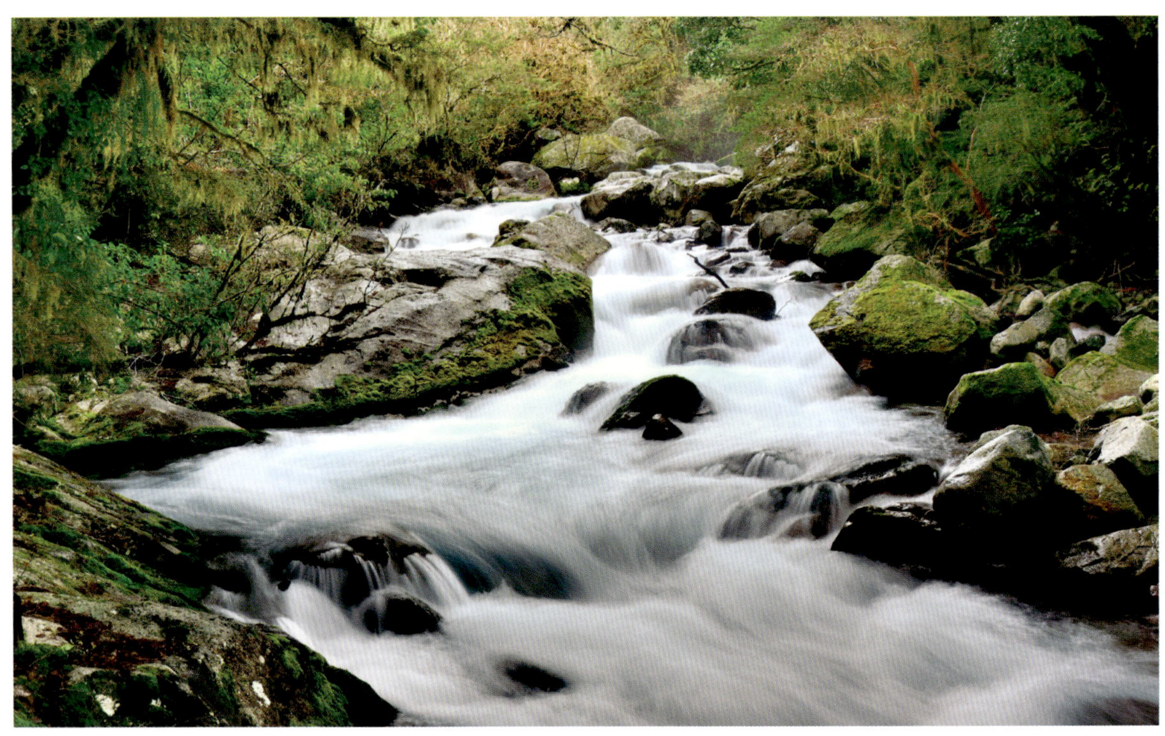

The Cascades, Lake Marian Track

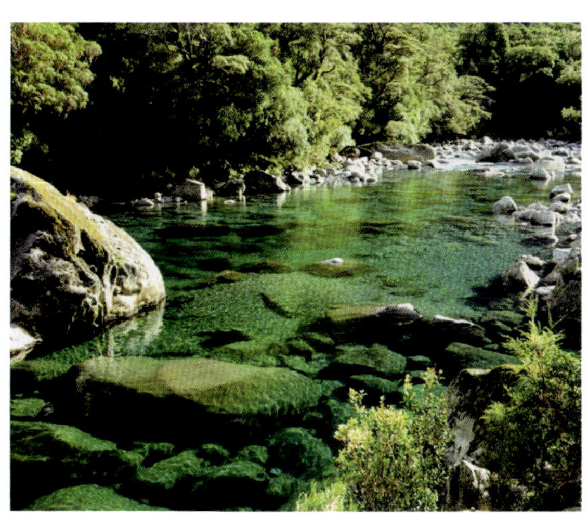

Cleddau River, near Milford Sound / Piopiotahi

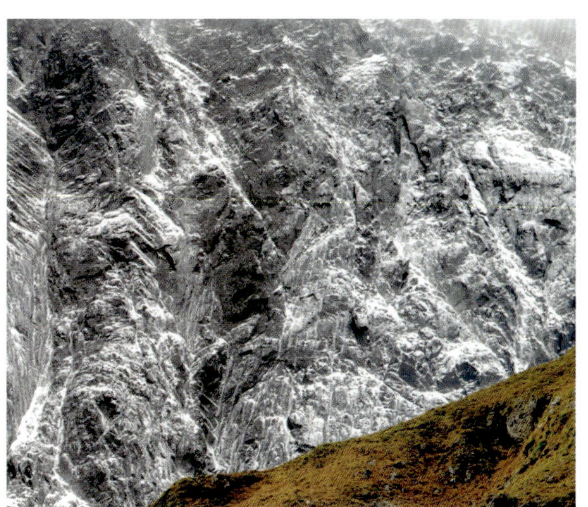

Mountainside, near the Homer Tunnel

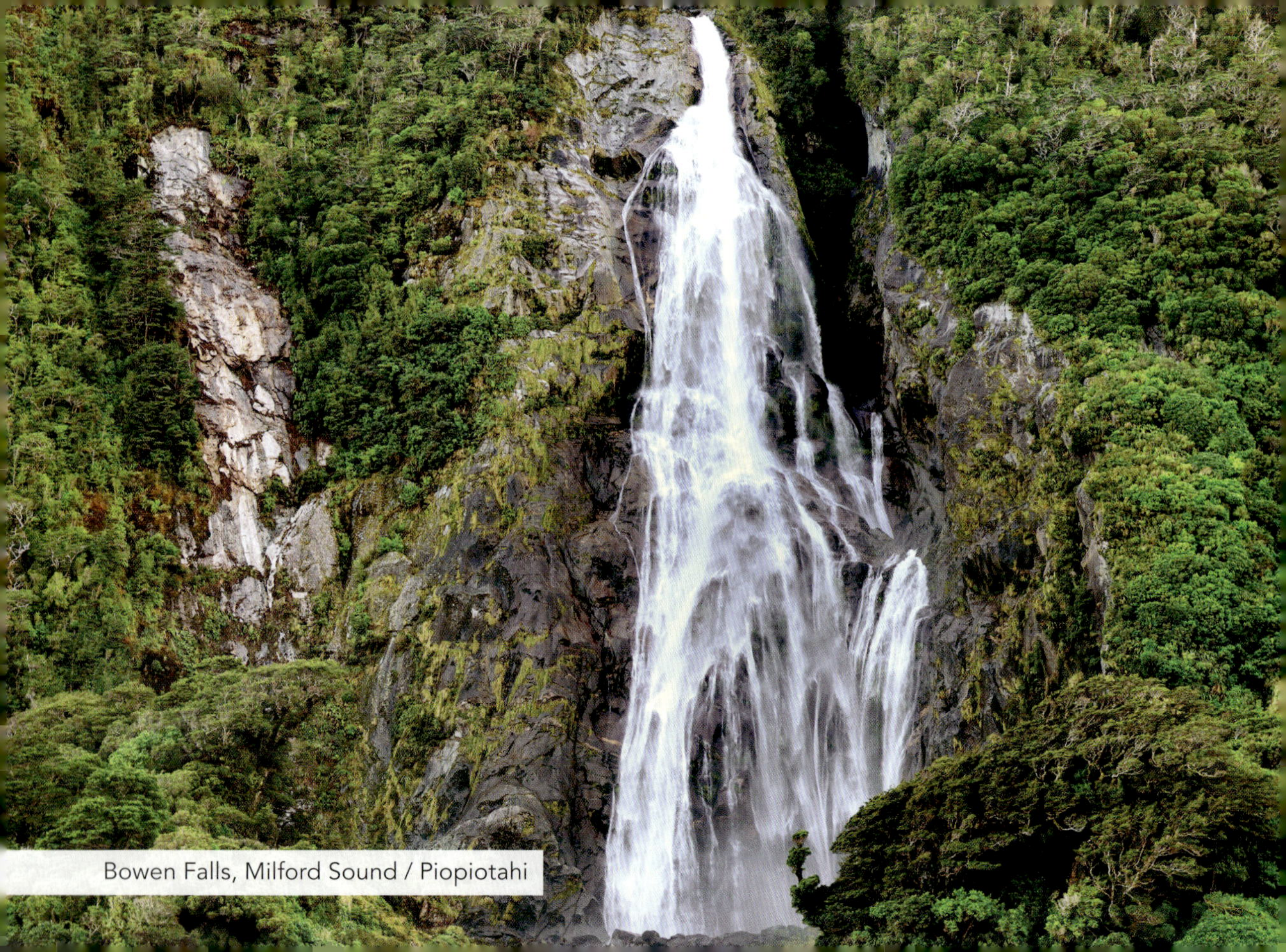

Bowen Falls, Milford Sound / Piopiotahi

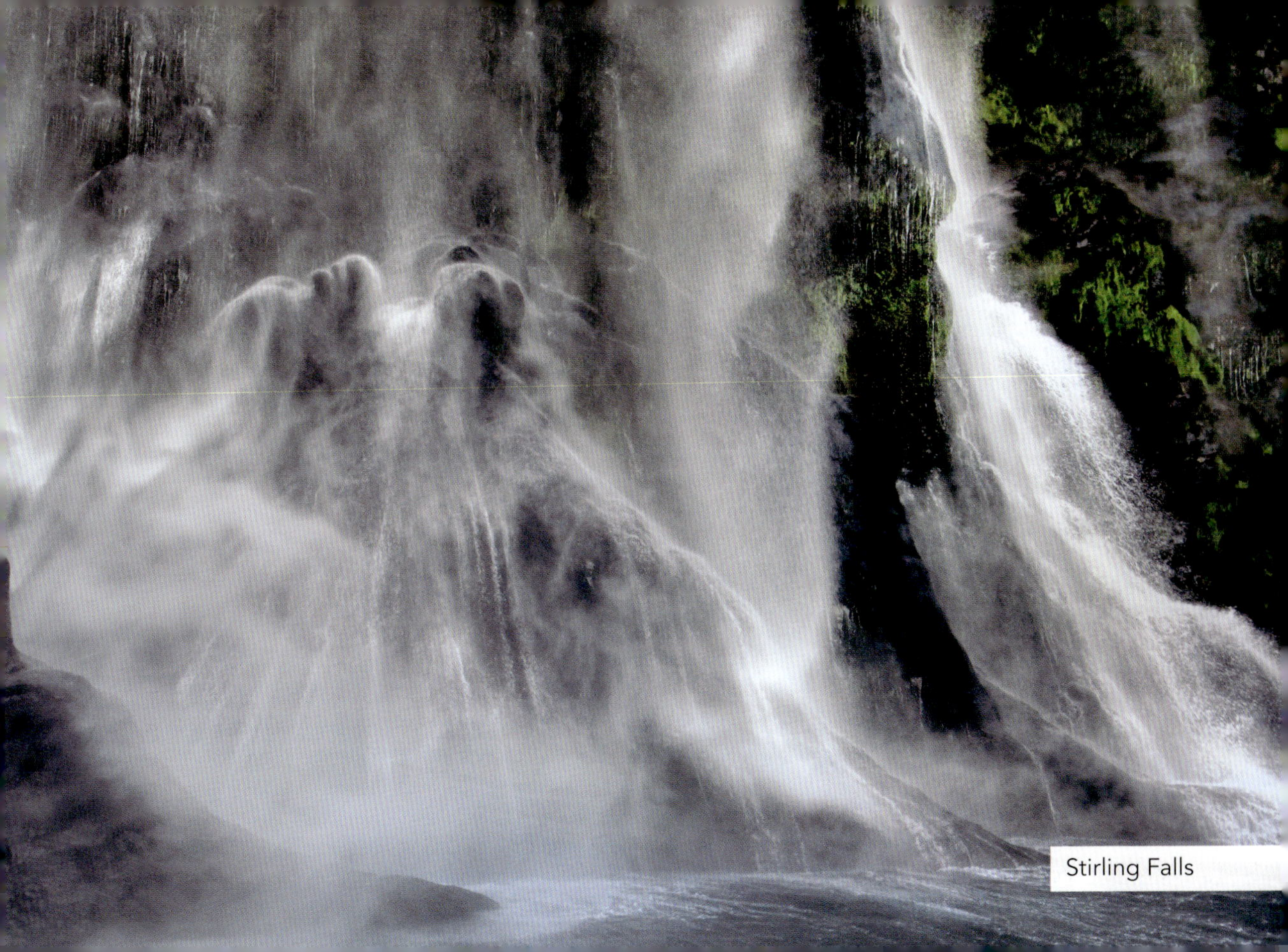

Stirling Falls

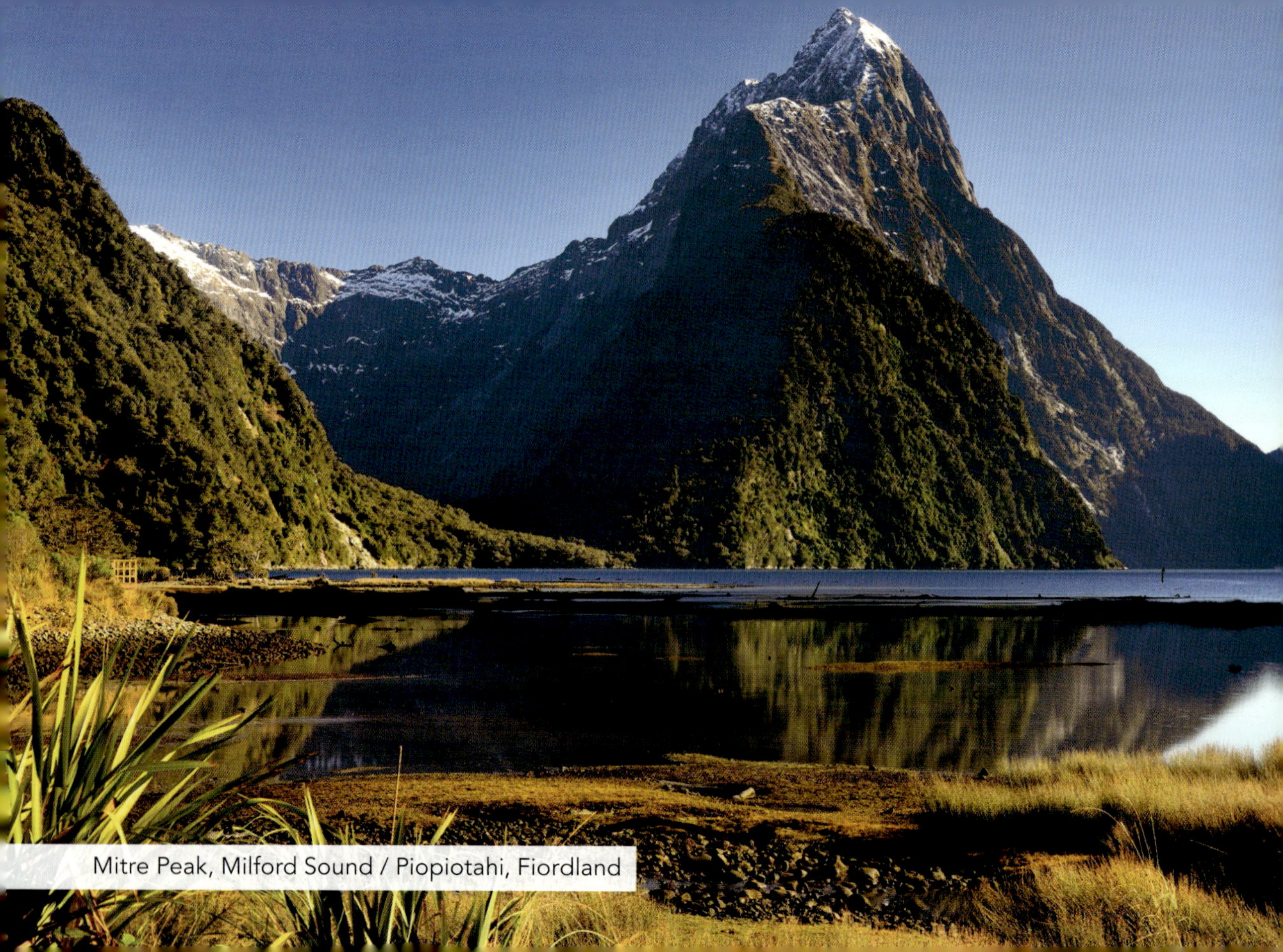

Mitre Peak, Milford Sound / Piopiotahi, Fiordland

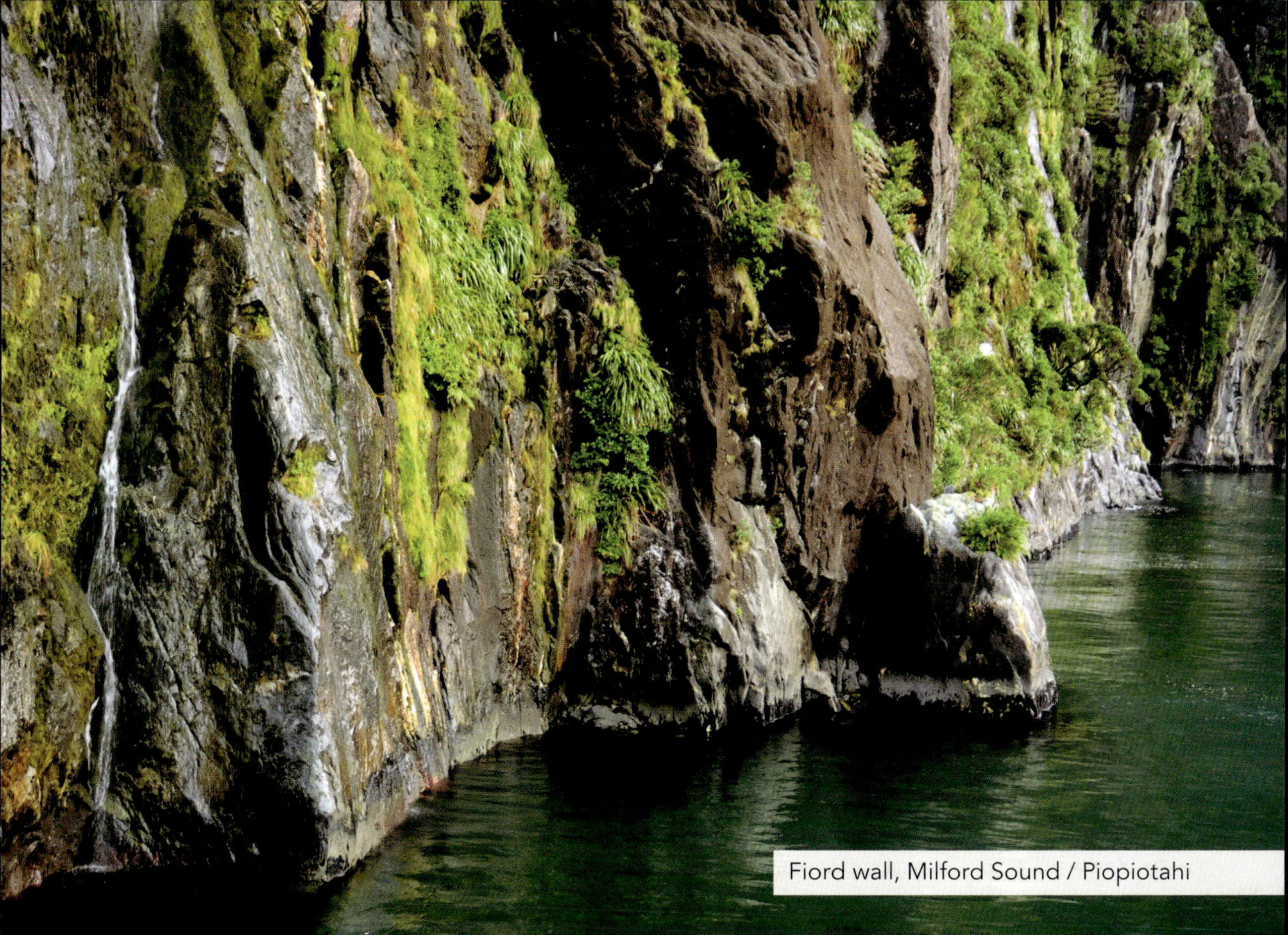

Fiord wall, Milford Sound / Piopiotahi

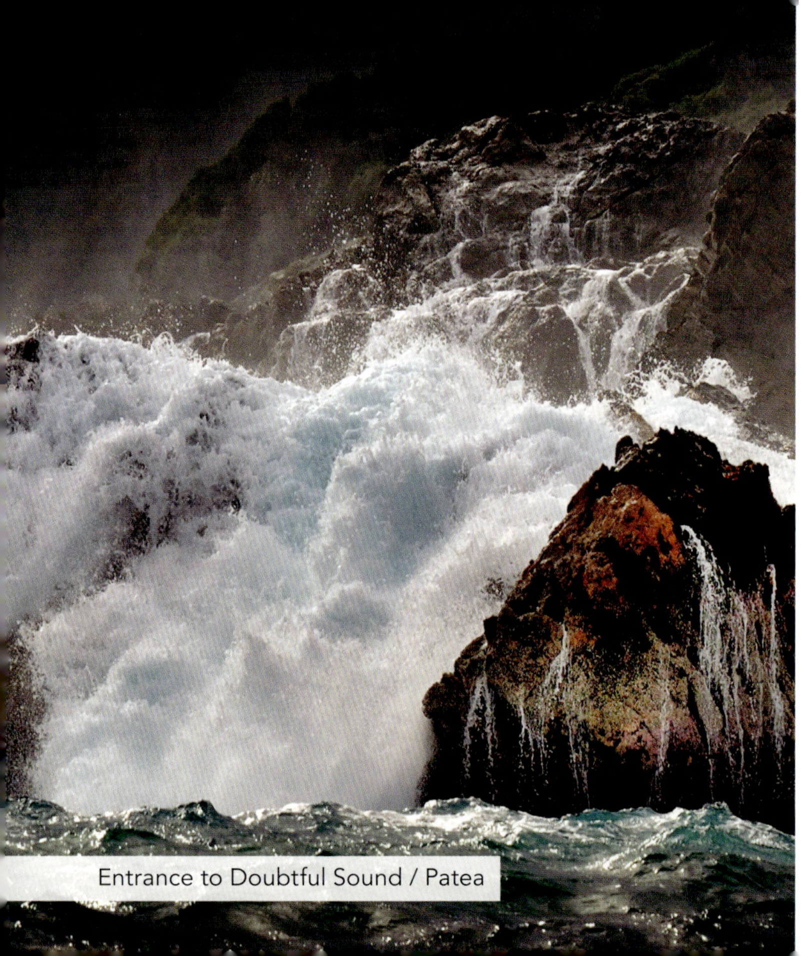

Entrance to Doubtful Sound / Patea

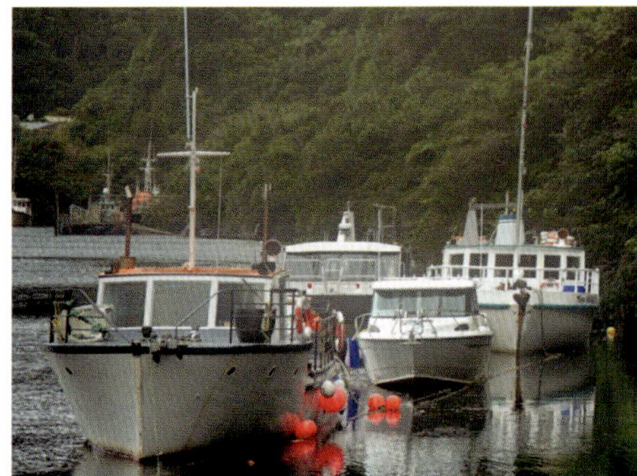

Deep Cove, Doubtful Sound / Patea

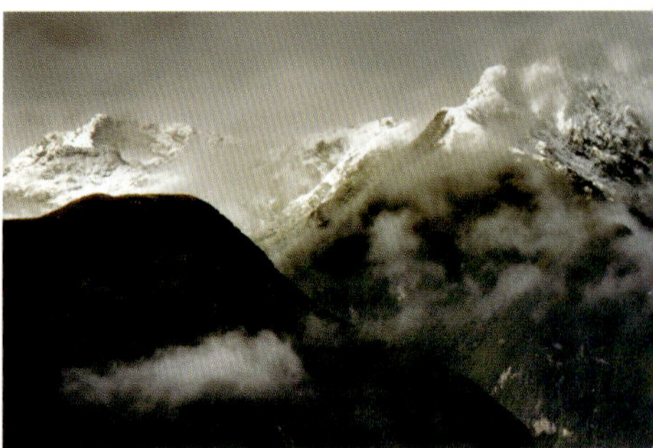

Mountainous entrance to Doubtful Sound / Patea

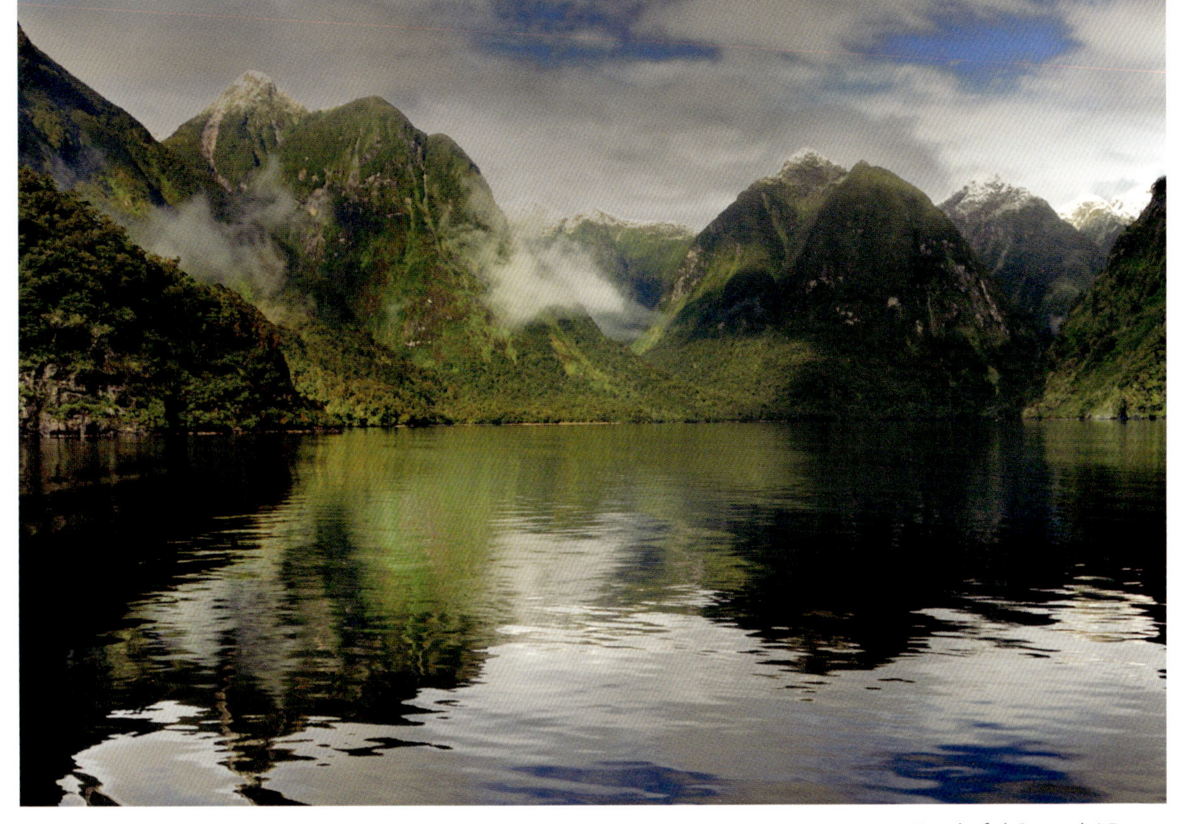

Doubtful Sound / Patea

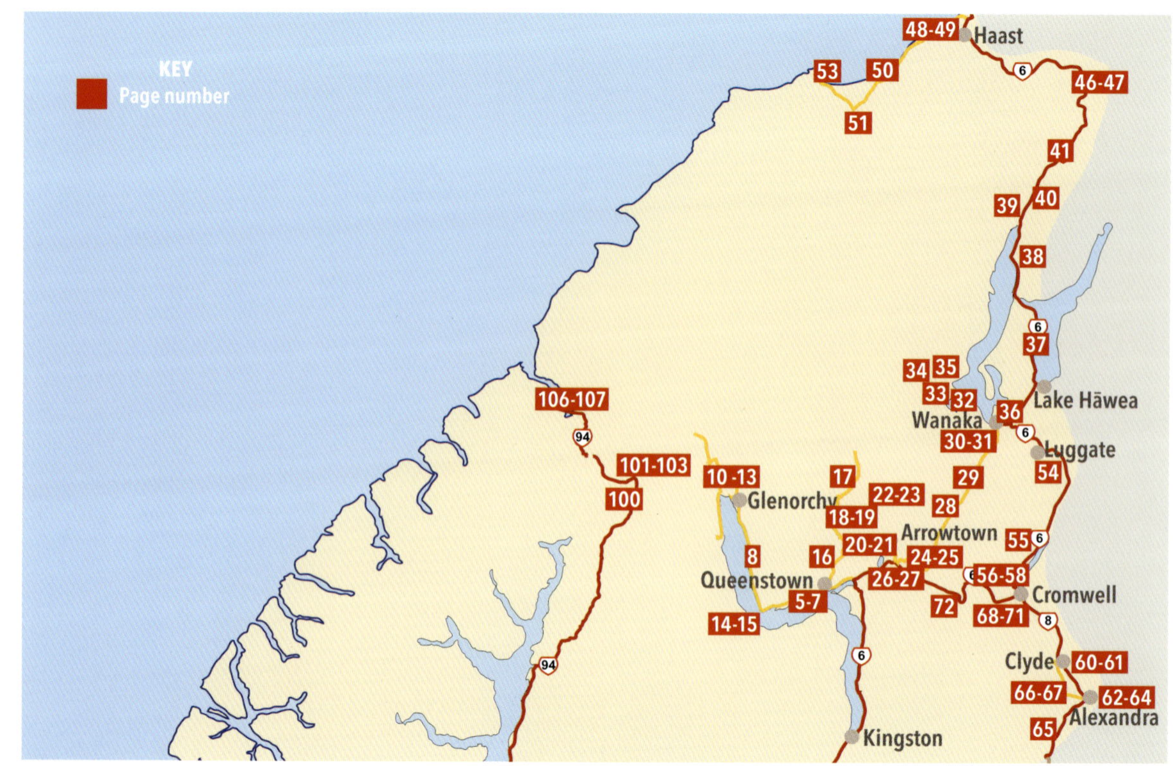
KEY
Page number
48-49
Haast
53
50
51
46-47
41
39
40
38
37
34
35
33
32
Lake Hāwea
36
Wanaka
30-31
Luggate
106-107
94
101-103
100
10-13
Glenorchy
17
22-23
29
28
54
18-19
Arrowtown
55
20-21
8
16
24-25
Queenstown
26-27
56-58
5-7
Cromwell
14-15
72
68-71
Clyde
60-61
66-67
62-64
Alexandra
65
Kingston
6
8

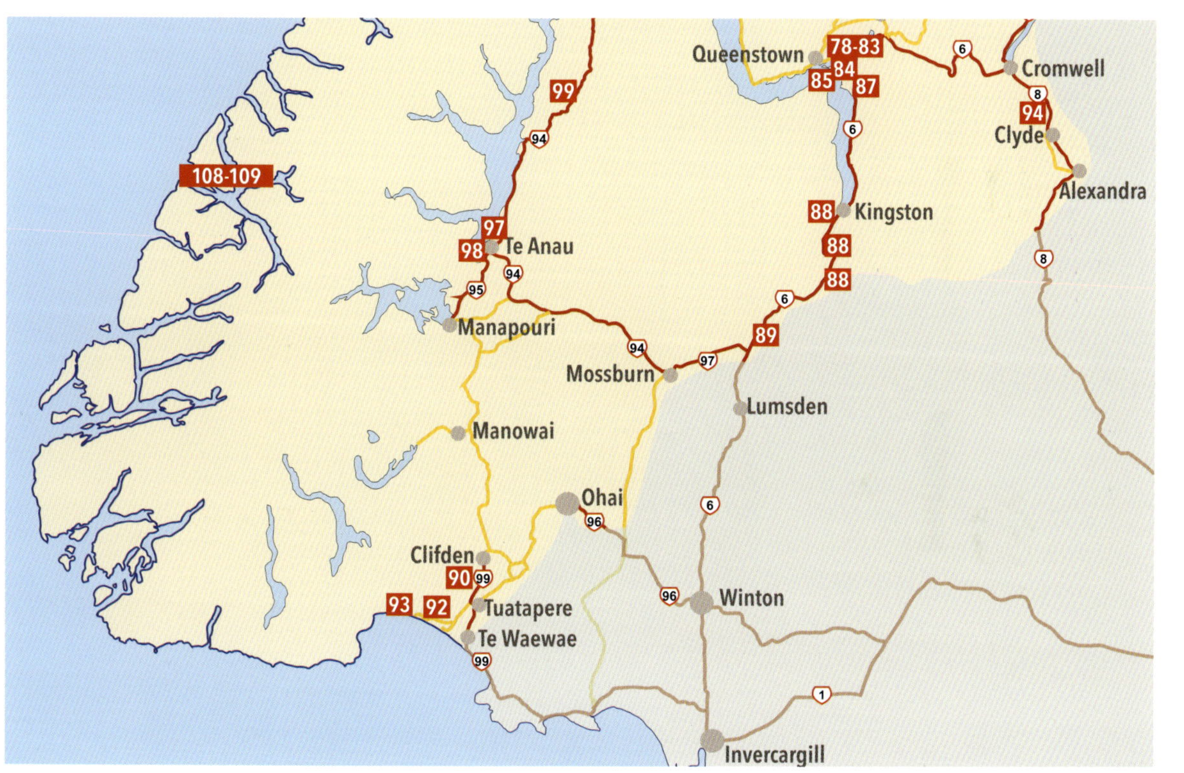

Queenstown
78-83
84
85
87
Cromwell
6
8
94
Clyde
Alexandra
99
94
108-109
97
98
Te Anau
94
95
88
Kingston
88
88
6
89
Manapouri
94
97
Mossburn
Lumsden
Manowai
Ohai
96
6
Clifden
90
99
93
92
Tuatapere
Te Waewae
99
96
Winton
1
Invercargill

112

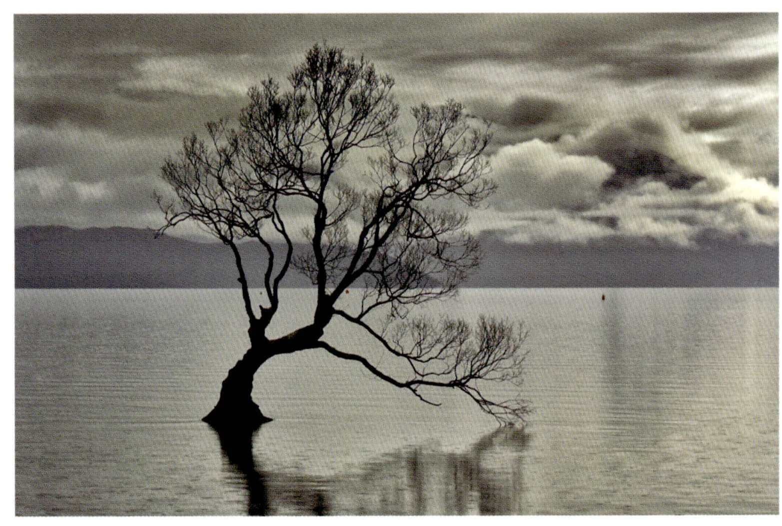

The Wānaka Tree
Roys Bay, Lake Wānaka

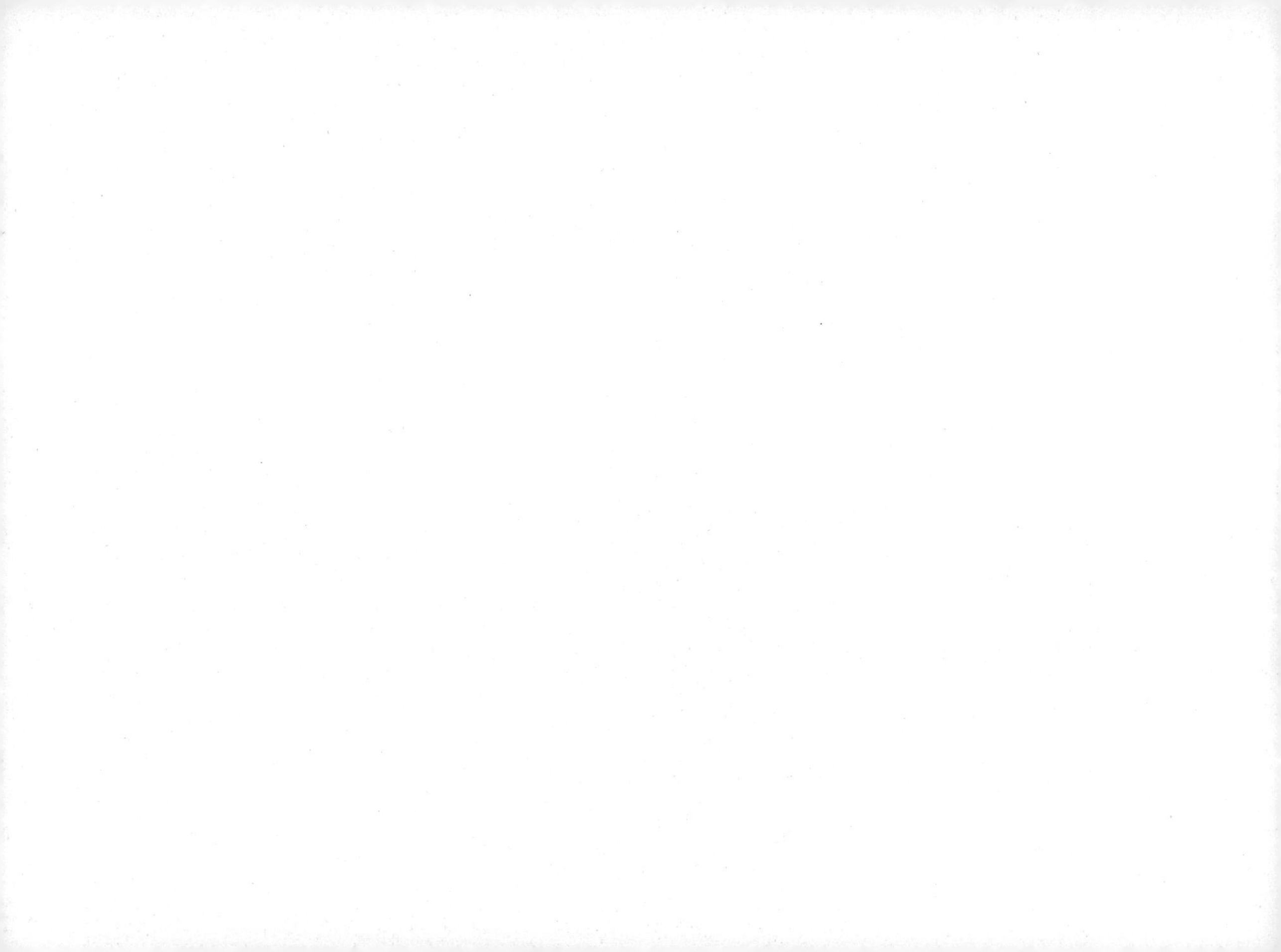